Lefka

today and yesterday

**A complete guide for travellers
with 204 colour illustrations
and maps**

EDITIONS
TOUBIS ®
ΕΚΔΟΣΕΙΣ

Texts: J. VOGIATZIS
Translation: G. COX, J. SOLMAN
Maps: NORADRAMITINOU - ANASTASOGLOU
Photographs: L. AGGELOPOULOS. J. VOGIATZIS, G. DESPIPRIS, L.
MERKATIS, M. TOUBIS, I. TIPALDOS, A. CHARAMOGLIS

Art Work: NORA DRAMITINOU - ANASTASOGLOU
Four-colour editing: YANNIS KOLLAROS
Photosetting: KIKI SANTORINAIOU
Montage: NIKOS PRASIANAKIS
Printed by: M. TOUBIS GRAPHIC ARTS S.A., Athens - Tel. no. 9923874

Our particular thanks to
L. MERKATI, I. TIPALDO and A. CHAMOGLI, all of Levkada, for the
contributions they have made to this book.

---

http://www.toubis.gr

3 - 98

Inset: the indigenous peony

THE SOIL
(extract)

O soil of my birthplace!
Soil of Lefkada,
the soil that first was,
the Titanic wellspring of my body
and of my unsleeping mind!

Angelos Sikelianos

Foreword

Lefkada's position among the famous and celebrated islands of the Ionian chain is a simple one, yet impossible to overlook. This is a verdant little place which Nature has blessed with contradictions that cannot but win the visitor's heart: the steep west coast consists of one superb beach after another, while on the east there are deep-shadowed bays where the woods run down to the water's edge, and in the centre winding roads connect stone-built villages in the traditional style.

Lefkada is island and mainland together, East and West side by side, and the length of its history allows it even to claim the honour of giving birth to Odysseus. Its medieval castle still stands today, mute but incontrovertible witness to the centuries of history that have gone into the making of the soul of each Lefkadan.

Here tradition and tourist development blend closely and harmoniously, a challenge to see things at closer quarters. Our guides, as ever, will be the Lefkadans themselves, whose courtesy, kindess, culture, exuberance and vitality win over every visitor and call us back again and again to this island close against the mainland shore.

In preparing this guide, our purpose has been to show readers something of the place which gave birth to Angelos Sikelianos of the Delphi Festival and the national hero and poet Aristotelis Valaoritis. But this is only the start: there is still much, much more to discover as one wanders the length and breadth of the island in search of the stuff of memories.

Index

Foreword... 4

**Geographical position
and Morphology**........................... 6
Map of the island........................... 8

HISTORY.................................... 10
Lefkada of Ithaca?........................ 12
The Ancient period....................... 13
The Roman period......................... 14
The Byzantine period.................... 15
Turks and Venetians..................... 17
Venetian rule................................ 17
French, Russians and British.......... 20
Liberation and After...................... 22

YESTERDAY AND TODAY...... 27

A TOUR OF THE ISLAND........ 56

**THE TOWN
OF LEFKADA**............................ 58
Town plan..................................... 70

ROUTES ON THE ISLAND...... 85

ROUTE 1
Faneromeni Monastery-
Ayios Nikitas-Kathisma-
Kalamitsi...................................... 86

ROUTE 2
Lazarata-Hortate-Athani-
Egremni-Porto Katsiki-
Cape Lefkatas............................... 97

ROUTE 3
(The centre of the island)
Lefkada-Karya-
Englouvi-Platystoma-
Vafkeri-Alexandros.....................106

ROUTE 4
Lefkada-Nikiana-Nidri.................112

Short trips from Nidri...............122
1: The Waterfall..........................122
2: St Kyriake..............................124
3: Niochori.................................125

The Nearby islands...................126
Madouri, Skorpios........................127
Meganisi....................................128

ROULE 5
Nidri-Poros-Syvota-
Vasiliki...................................... 130

Short trips from Vasiliki...........140
Syvros-Ayios Petros....................140

Bibliographe...............................142
Useful information.......................143
Hotels.......................................143

Geographical Position and Morphology

Lefkada is an island in the Ionian Sea; one of the "Eptanisa" - "Seven Islands", it is about halfway along the western seaboard of Greece.

Like the other Ionian Islands, Lefkada is situated in an area of tectonic rifts. Indeed, to the west of the island is the Great Ionian Rift, which accounts for the great depth of the sea off the west coast of the islands and their sharply plunging shoreline on that side.

Earthquakes have shaken the area on a number of occasions since antiquity, and many of them —such as those of 1825 and 1948, to refer only to modern history— have been most destructive. Even today, tremors are occsionally felt in and around Lefkada.

The climate of the island is on the Mediterranean type. There is prolonged sunshine, and cloud-cover levels are low. The winter is mild, with relatively high air temperatures, more frequent rain and occasional frost or snow. The summer is warm, though there are cool breezes which keep down the humidity.

Springs of water are rare on Lefkada, and are mostly confined to the east and south. There are no extensive forests; the Aleppo pine grows by self-seeding in the south and on the surrounding islets, while the cypress is the most common conifer. Among deciduous trees, the oak and the plane are widespread. Scrub is most plentiful in the southern part of the island.

Unusually in Greece, two species of peony (*Paeonia peregrina* and *P. mascula*) are both found on Lefkada. there are small but interesting woods of the *Quercus cessiliflora* oak on Mt Skaros and near the village of Kollyvata.

The most interesting ecological phenomenon on the island is, perhaps, the wetland of the lagoon near the town. From the botanical point of view, there is a wide range of water-loving trees, bushes and reeds, and the fauna, too, is varied, with numerous rare migratory and indigenous birds (including pelicans, herons, wild duck and wild geese).

The steep western coast ends at towering Cape Lefkatas.

The strange geological formations of Meganisi make for impressive natural settings.

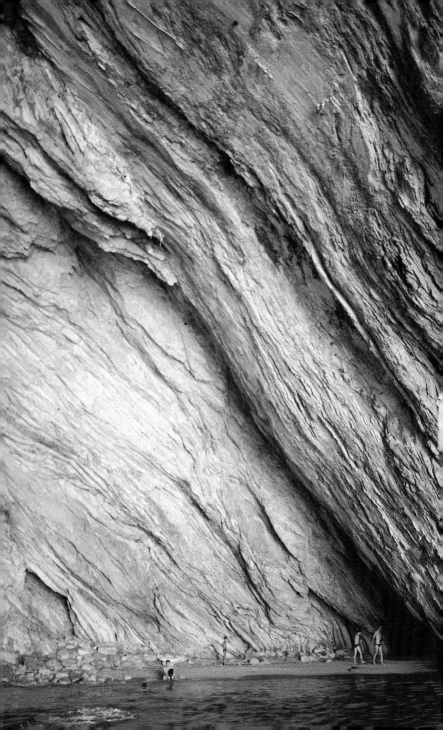

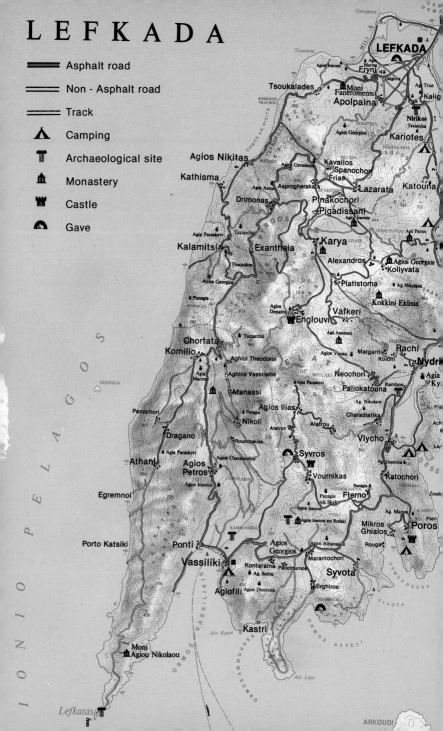

LEFKADA

▬▬▬	Asphalt road
═══	Non - Asphalt road
▭▭▭	Track
⛺	Camping
🏛	Archaeological site
🏛	Monastery
♜	Castle
⌂	Gave

The island lies at a distance of 78 metres from the mainland coast of Akarnania. In effect, the island is separated from the rest of Greece by the Lefkada channel, which has a width of 25 metres and is spanned by a floating bridge.

With an area of 305.21 square kilometres, Lefkada is the fourth-largest of the Ionian Islands, after Cephalonia, Corfu and Zakynthos. Administratively, it and its nine accompanying islets (Meganisi or Tafos, Kalamos, Kastos, Skorpios, Skorpidi, Madouri, Sparti, Thileia and Kythros) make up the smallest Greek Prefecture in terms both of population and area. The capital of the Prefecture is the town of Lefkada itself.

The population of the Prefecture is 23,000, and it consists of one sub-prefecture with three municipalities and 40 communes.

The island of Lefkada is largely mountainous (72.6% of its ground is mountainous, 17.2% is semi-mountainous and only 10.2% is low-lying). From the central massif, whose main peaks are Stavrota (1,182 m), Ayios Ilias (1,040 m), Pyrgos (1,058 m) and Mega Oros (1,012 m) lower ranges (Lainaki, Achrada, Sikero, Skaroi, Megali Rachi, Lefkata peninsula) plunge sharply into the sea and form the steep and rocky coastline.

High up in the mountains, and between the ranges of lower hills, are narrow plateaus at different altitudes (Kalokairino, Sfakiotis, Lefkata, etc.). The hills also form valleys, the largest of which is that at Vasiliki. To the north of the island is Lefkada's only real plain, around the main town.

There are no proper rivers, just seasonal torrents whose steep sides give them the nature of gorges or ravines.

HISTORY

The island —to distinguish it from the town— was known as Leucadia in antiquity. The name 'Leucas' or 'Lefkas' comes from the adjective 'leucos', meaning 'white'. At the southernmost extremity of the island, towering white cliffs lead down to the famous Cape Lefkatas (known today as Doukato and in ancient times as Lefkas Petra or Lefkas Akra), which had the sailors of antiquity in fear and trembling. Homer locates one of the entries to the Underworld here. On the cape stood an ancient temple of Apollo, and according to the traditions it was here that the poetess Sappho flung herself into the sea in her grief when Phaon rejected her love (see p. 103).

In the very first period of human civilisation, Lefkada was part of the adjacent mainland, as were the rest of the Ionian Islands. In 1967, excavations conducted by A. Sordinas brought to light flint tools dating from the Palaeolithic period (8000 BC) at sites all the way from the northernmost point on the island (near Tsoukalades) to the far south (near Evyiros).

Finds from the Neolithic period (c. 4000 BC) had already been discovered by Dörpfeld in the 'Choirospilia' cave near Evyiros (see p. 129). More indications of a human presence in this period were found in the 'Asvospilia' cave near Frini, not far f rom the town, and in 1965 a Neolithic axe came to light on Meganisi.

Close contact with the inhabitants of the coastline of Epirus —and with those of Italy— continued in the early Bronze Age. It may have been these same people who later, in the middle Bronze Age, developed the unique culture of which traces have been found near Nidri. Links can also be hypothesised with the mythical Teleboans, one of whose centres —perhaps the most important— was the island of Taphos, today called Meganisi. The Taphians were famed as sailors and pirates.

Two centuries after occupying the Ionian Islands, the Teleboans —according to the myths — moved further south and staked their claim on the power of golden Mycenae. In the battle which followed, the King of Mycenae lost seven of his eight sons. His nephew, Amphitryon, undertook to avenge him: with his allies Cephalus of Attica, Panopeus of Phocis and Eleius of the Argolid, he conquered the islands and gave them to Cephalus and Eleius, who settled there. And Cephalus begat Arkeisius and Arkeisius begat Laertes, who was the father of Homer's Odysseus.

The power of the Teleboans was followed by that of the Cephallenes. One memory of their control over Lefkada is preserved in the myth that Laertes, one of the legendary leaders of the Cephallenes, conquered Nericus, on the 'coast of Epirus', which has been identified with Lefkada. However, the principal mythical figure of the Cephallenes was Odysseus, who led their detachment in the Trojan War, which fell towards the end of the Mycenean period. Laertes married his son Odysseus to Penelope, giving her father, Icarius, the island of Lefkada (which was not then known by that name) as a gift.

In the plain of Nidri, archaeological excavations have brought to light traces of an extensive early Bronze Age settlement (c. 2000 BC), with tombs and the foundations of circular buildings.

*An engraving showing Sappho on the cliffs at Lefkatas before the plunge
into the sea (from the periodical Esperos, 1889)*

The Homeric Enigma: Lefkada or Ithaca?

The identification of Lefkada with Homer's Ithaca has been the object of much academic controversy. However, Homer describes the landscape of his hero's homeland in such a way as to make it impossible, for the present, to place it finally and beyond doubt in the modern geographical context.

The poet places Ithaca in a group of islands: Ithaca, Duliche and Same. But which is which? And is Lefkada one of them? Geography has its part to play here, since if in antiquity the Lefkada channel did not exist and the island was part of the mainland, Homer would not have called it an island. In the 1st century, Strabo tells us that until the Corinthians dug the channel in 650 BC (see p. 13), Lefkada was joined to the mainland. Perhaps, though, all the Corinthians did was to dig out a channel which had been blocked by silt. The argument advanced by the 19th century traveller Leake that Lefkada must have been as much or as little of an island in antiqity as it is in modern times seems logical, but does not help very much.

The dispute —which began even in ancient times— was revived towards the end of the 19th century when the discoveries of Heinrich Schliemann at Troy and Mycenae persuaded an amazed world that the Homeric epics were based on historical fact. Historians began once again to look at the stops on Odysseus's voyage home, since apart from the purely mythical locations in the Mediterranean there were also real places which the spades of archaeologists might be able to reveal. It might even prove possible to find Odysseus's palace.

In 1878, Schliemann began investigating modern Ithaki, and the finds produced during his brief dig there led him to identify the island with ancient Ithaca. But his assistant Dörpfeld, who continued his excavations, used the text of the Odyssey as a basis for identifying Homer's Ithaca with modern Lefkada. He placed Odysseus's palace near Nidri, where he began to dig.

The most important —and most obscure— reference to Ithaca in Homer is to be found in the Odyssey, Book IX, 21-27, where Odysseus describes his homeland to King Alcinous of the Phaeacians:

My home is under the clear skies of Ithaca.
Our landmark is the wooded peak of windswept Neriton.
For neighbours we have many peopled isles
with no great space between them,
Dulichium and Same and wooded Zacynthus.
But Ithaca, the farthest out to sea,
lies slanting to the west, whereas the others
face the dawn and the rising sun.

Although many attempts have been made to recognise and locate the real places described in the Odyssey - whether in Ithaki or Lefkada -—none of the conflicting theories has yet been confirmed, since this could only be done by means of archaeological evidence which has so far not appeared.

Lefkada crowning Corinth, 1873 (from Kavadias' "Excavations at Corinth".

The Ancient Period

In the period following the collapse of the Mycenean civilisation, the inhabitants of this part of Greece began to regroup around the island of Karnos (modern Kalamos), which gave its name to a new nation: the Akarnanians. Their sphere of influence also included Lefkada, whose inhabitants were known as 'Epileucadians'.

By the 7th century BC Lefkada had an important city, Nericus. which lay a little to the south of the modern capital, near the village of Kallithea. At one time, it was possible to follow the walls of the ancient city "for more than 2,500 paces" and the turrets at the corners could be picked out. The length of the walls is an indication that this must have been one of the largest ancient Greek cities. But modern agricultural and housing development has allowed only a few traces of ancient Nericus to survive, and the an-

cient theatre, which was excavated by Dörpfeld, has almost completely disappeared.

In the 7th century, Corinth —the greatest power in the western seas— snatched Lefkada from the Akarnanians by guile. It may have been they who founded the city of Leucas, near Nericus; in any case, it was their principal base in the Ambracian Gulf area and on the sea route to Sicily, Lower Italy and the Adriatic. In order to make their defences more effective, the Corinthian colonists dug —or perhaps simply widened— the channel between Lefkada and the mainland. They built a bridge over the canal thus formed: a bridge which, as the Roman historian Livy tells us, had a length of 500 paces and a breadth of 125. At this time, the population of the island was 20,000, an indication of its prosperity.

On the coast opposite, the Corinthians built the settlement of Sollion. This was not an independent city, but was subject to Leucas and to Anaktorio, their other colony in Akarnania. The ruined ancient fortifications beneath and around the more recent castle of St George must be those of Sollion. Throughout the centuries which followed, Leucas remained loyal to its Corinthian roots, although it regarded itself as an independent state which simply maintained friendly relations with the mother-city.

Leucas took part in the battle of Salamis against the Persians in 480 BC. It sent three ships, which actually arrived in time for the battle, which is more than can be said for neighbouring Corfu, also a Corinthian colony. And at the battle of Plataea, which saw the end of the Persian menace, there were 800 "men of Leucas and Ambracia".

In 431 BC the Peloponnesian War broke out, splitting the Greek world in two as the city-states aligned themselves with either Sparta or Athens, the two protagonists. Corinth went with Sparta, and Leucas followed it.

Leucas sent ships to join the Corinthian fleet which was victorious in battle against the Athenians under their admiral Phormion, and one of them was sunk. In 428 BC, Asopius, son of Phormion, punished Leucas for this by looting it, but he was killed and a part of his army annihilated as they left the island.

Leucas also sent ships to help Sparta during the abortive Athenian campaign in Sicily.

Although Leucas was on the winning side in the Peloponnesian War, the fighting seriously damaged the island. Nonetheless, it enjoyed two more centuries of prestige.

In 337 BC the leadership of the Greek world was taken over by Philip of Macedon, who was elected general and emperor. After his assassination, he was succeeded by Alexander the Great, who united the Greek cities (and Leucas) for the campaign against the Persians.

When Alexander died in 323 BC, Leucas broke away from his empire and allied itself with Athens.

Although Alexander's successors occupied the island, it revolted once more in 312 BC and declared itself independent.

The Roman Period

Until the 3rd century BC, there were two basic relationships which deter-

A Lefkadan stater, 400-330 BC.

mined the history of Lefkada. On the one hand, as a dependency of the mother-city Corinth it took part in all the conflicts in which the atter was involved, either locally in the Ionian area or more generally (e.g. the Persian Wars).

On the other hand, it attempted to resist the constant pressure of its Akarnanian neighbours on the mainland, whose policy was aimed primarily at bringing the city (and the island) within its federated state, thus restoring the unity of Akarnania as a whole.

In the 3rd century, the Akarnanians were finally successful: Lefkada became a member of the 'Koinon of the Akarnanians' and for a while was even its capital. But in the next century, the growing power of Rome, seeing that the unity of Lefkada and the mainland was strengthening local resistance to its rule, made Lefkada 'independent' once more, separating it from the Koinon of the Akarnanians.

During the wars between Rome and Macedon, which began in about 230 BC, the Akarnanians of the mainland, who still thought of Lefkada as their capital, decided to fight with Macedon, despite the fact that they had clearly chosen the losing side. Titus Quintus Flaminius, commander of the Roman forces —who happened to be in Corfu at the time— decided that his reprisals should take the form of laying siege to Lefkada. This siege was a major military undertaking and one of the most important events ever to have happened on the island. The islanders put up a heroic resistance, but they were betrayed by Italian refugees who lived in the town. The fighting was very fierce, and it ended with the destruction of the ancient city.

We have very little information about the effect which the Roman period had on the island, although we know that there was much building of public works (walls, fortresses, bridges). But the balance of power shifted perceptibly from the island to the new city of Nikopolis, which was founded on the mainland after the battle of Actium in 31 BC. The new city drew its inhabitants from Lefkada and the surrounding area, and it was decorated with art works looted from nearby cities and towns.

The most interesting conclusion to be drawn about the ancient history of Lefkada is that the island and the mainland facing it constituted an economic, geographical and social unit. This unity was a prerequisite for prosperity in the region as a whole, and the attempts to break it up were designed precisely to weaken the area and allow it to be controlled as two districts.

The Byzantine Period

We know little more about the Byzantine period than we do about Roman rule. There must have been a Christian bishop of Lefkada, though, since one took part in the Council of Nicaea in 325.

In the 5th century, Lefkada was sacked by the Vandals and the Huns, and in the mid-6th century two severe earthquakes had a damaging effect on the island's development.

We hear of a Bishop of Lefkada once more in 968, when Ambassador Liutprado, Bishop of Cremona, stayed with him for a few days on his way to Constantinople. After the 6th century Lefkada was incorporated into the Byzantine 'theme' (administrative district) of the Ionian, which was administered from Cephallonia. Relations with the mainland were only interrupted temporarily, as was the case with the raids of the forces of Pisa in 1099 and 1103.

In 1204, Constantinople, capital of the Byzantine Empire, fell to the 'flower of chivalry': the Crusaders. The Crusades had supposedly begun as an attempt to liberate the Holy Land, but in effect the main concern of the knights was to 'liberate' any thing that came to hand. The Byzantine Empire broke up for a while, reformed, and was finally overthrown by the Turks in 1453. For many parts of southern and western Greece, the Crusades ushered in a long period of subjugation to foreign princes, but throughout this troubled period Lefkada followed the fortunes of the Despotate of Epirus.

The victorious 'Frankish' potentates divided up Greece amongst themselves. One quarter of Constanti-

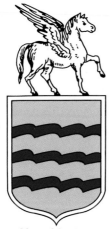

The emblem of the Counts Tocci

The emblem of Duke Walter

The emblem of the Counts de Orsini

noble itself and 3/8 of the Empire, including the Ionian Islands, went to the Venetians; but because the Venetian state was unable to maintain control over all these new lands, it announced its intention of conceding them to individual Venetians or friends of Venice, on condition that they recognised Venetian sovereignty. It took Lefkada almost a century to come under Venetian rule, since for a while the Despotate of Epirus, a Greek principality based on Ioannina, managed to keep a grip on north western Greece. But in 1293, Nicephorus Angelus I, a Despot (a term which at that time designated a ruler exercising royal power) of the Comnenus line, married his daughter to Giovanni Orsini and gave her Lefkada as her dowry. Orsini was the son of Roberto Orsini, lord of Cephallonia and Zakynthos. At this time, the whole area was subject to widespread piracy, and for that reason the new master of Lefkada requested —and received— permission to built a fortress to defend the island. This was the structure later to be known as Santa Maura castle.

A few years later, Giovanni Orsini succeeded his father, and was now Count of Cephallonia, Zakynthos, Ithaca and Lefkada.

Throughout the 14th century, there were constant changes of government and the island was bought and sold a number of times or given to newly-arrived nobles who imposed ruthless taxes to increase their profits.

The De Tocci dynasty introduced a certain amount of stability, but a new threat appeared at the end of the 15th century: the Turks, who after capturing Constantinople had advanced slowly but steadily across the rest of Greece.

Turks and Venetians

The only Western state capable of - or interested in - resisting the Turkish advance across Greek territory, and thus into Europe, was Venice. Thus the 16th and 17th centuries were taken up by wars between the Serene Republic of Venice and Turkey. These wars swung now one way and now the other, but they were of course never to the benefit of the impoverished Greeks whose lands both sides were claiming.

In 1479, a fleet of 29 Turkish ships under Geduk Ahmet Pasha took Lefkada without encountering any resistance from the Venetians. The Pasha took most of the islanders as prisoners, and sold them as slaves in the bazaars of Smyrna and Constantinople, while his soldiers looted and vandalised the island.

In 1502, Lefkada changed hands once again, when a surprise Venetian attack overcame the castle garrison. But it went back to the Turks by treaty in 1503, and was to remain in their possession for the next 180 years.

There is little information about conditions on the island in this period. Because of its geographical position, with good harbours and numerous surrounding islets, Lefkada was a natural haunt for the pirates of the Ionian Sea and the area around it was one of the most hazardous for ordinary shipping. The pirates whose lair was Santa Maura preyed most on the ships from the other —Venetian owned— Ionian islands, which is why the local Turkish administration usually co-operated with them rather than trying to stamp them out.

Apart from the fact that they built the Ayia Marina aqueduct — the most important piece of public building done during the entire period— Turkish rule had only negative consequences for the island. Most of the fertile land (some 3/5 of the total number of fields) was held by a small number of Turks, yet thanks to their industriousness the local Greeks were able to cultivate almost double the quantity of grapes and olives. The overall economic position was poor, however. The drunken pirate crews who roamed the town, the severities of the tax-farming system, the periods of forced labour and the tragedy of the Christian children carried off to be trained as janissaries brought the people of Lefkada to despair.

Venetian Rule

In 1684, the Venetians organised a fresh attack on Lefkada, and the islanders greeted their new rulers with relief and even enthusiasm, although the motives of the Venetians were anything but noble. The operation was commanded by Francesco Morosini, the leading Venetian soldier of his day (among his less praiseworthy exploits was the partial destruction of the Athens Acropolis). After a siege of 16 days —during which the Venetians were amazed to see the arrival, to help them, of Timothy, Bishop of Cephallonia, with a detachment of 150 heavily-armed priests and monks— the castle fell and the Turks retreated to the mainland.

Lefkada was ruled by Venice from 1684 to 1797, with a brief interruption in 1715 when the Turks re-captured it for less than a year. Prolonged Venetian rule, which had a decisive impact at the time and some of whose effects

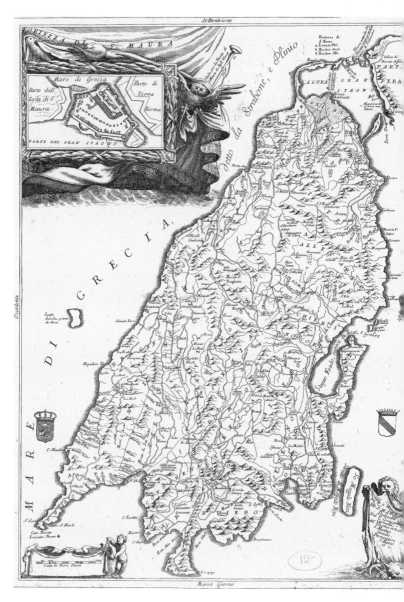

A map of Lefkada from an engraving of 1687, taken from Coronelli's Isolario; in the inset,
a plan of the castle of Santa Maura (see p. 62).

can still be seen today, is one of the most important events in the island's history.

To begin with, it seemed that better days had at last come to Lefkada: almost at once, the Venetians gave the island a rudimentary constitution, and a limited amount of self-government. Of particular importance was the transferring of the capital from inside the castle to the current site, then occupied by the district known as the 'Amaxiti'. But the new town, built on the marsh which backed the lagoon, had no harbour and trade remained in the hands of the Venetians who lived in the harbour. There was not even any real gain in terms of ease of communication with the villages of the hinterland.

As a result, rural life remained on a low level, and the townspeople, too, sank into decline. The 'buranellos', or Lefkadan townsman of the new type, came to symbolise the moral and economic collapse of what had been a flourishing settlement. Throughout the Venetian period, nonetheless, the contrast between the debased townspeople and the poor villagers remained.

In 1699 there was an influx of colonists from Crete, and a few years later a wave of refugees from Turkish-occupied Greece. But when hostilities broke out once more between the Ottoman Empire and Venice, in 1715,the Venetians abandoned Lefkada to its fate. The Turks entered the town, slaughtered many of its inhabitants and stayed for a year. They withdrew from the shattered town only when a Venetian fleet was sighted off the island in 1716.

The most important thing which the second period of Venetian rule gave Lefkada was a life of relative peace and security, in which the islanders could cultivate the land which was their fathers' inheritance. The pirate raids which had once been so frequent almost stopped, and the sudden movements of population came to an end.

Lefkada remained in the hands of the Venetians for the rest of the 18th century. The other Ionian islands had been in the Venetian empire for much longer: the occupation of Corfu dated back as far as 1386. On those islands, the Venetians had had much more time to mould society into the shape they wished. They were able to create a local aristocracy which owed them allegiance, the Italian language was widely used and many young people studied in Italy. None of this happened in Lefkada, however, as a result of which the island remained much more 'Greek' than Zakynthos or Corfu.

The intellectual life of Lefkada was relatively impoverished, as we can see from the absence of a tradition in poetry and urban folk song, which the islanders were forced to borrow from elsewhere. However, after 200 years of cultural and political isolation from the other Ionian islands, Lefkada now threw in its fate with them in a common course through history until the ultimate day of liberation and union with Greece.

Under the Venetians, Lefkada was for the first time governed in a rational manner and social and political life was relatively highly-organised in the town, which was much as we see it today. The fact that there were courts meant that there were lawyers, and they formed the nucleus of the island 'intelligentsia'. The first university graduates on Lefkada were notaries, pharmacists and doctors.

French, Russians and British

By the late 18th century Venice was a power in decline. Although it was not until 1796 that the Sublime Republic was actually overthrown (by Napoleon), it had begun to lose its Greek possessions, one by one, in the late 17th century. However, none of the European powers was prepared to see the Ionian islands pass into the hands of the Turks, and this created the problem of how they were to be governed, given that there was as yet no free Greek state into which they could be incorporated.

Since Lefkada and the other islands lay on the route east, they were an area of interest for the rival Great Powers. As a result Lefkada changed hands five times between 1797 and 1810. Three of the transfers of ownership were by war fought on its territory, with disastrous results for the island. Throughout this period the new ideas of the French Revolution made a profound impression on the ordinary people and particularly on the rural population, who sought to improve their position in society, and it was at this time that the foundations of an educational system for all the islanders were laid.

The French occupying forces held Lefkada for only two years (1797-1798), during which time the island was ruled by a Provisional Democratic Government with 24 members. After this, it passed into the hands of the Russians, whose strategic aim was to liberate the Balkans from the Turks and at the same time increase their own influence in the area. This period of occupation was a step backwards by comparison with the more liberal period of French rule.

The Lazare

A view of the Lefkada channel from t

...efkada (Joseph Cartwright, "Views in the Ionian Islands", London 1821).
...opolis of the ancient city, outside Kalligoni (Cartwright).

From 1800 to 1808, Lefkada was under Russian protection and formed part of the 'Seven Island State'. When the formation of this state was announced, its Constitution was drawn up in Constantinople (because Constantinople had once been the capital of the Byzantine Empire, this document was known as the 'Byzantine Constitution').

At about this time (1807) Lefkada was very nearly sold to the fearsome Ali Pasha of Ioannina, who needed it for use as a base for his operations against the Greek freedom-fighters who had appeared in the mountains of Central Greece and Epirus. The plan to hand Lefkada over to Ali Pasha was scotched at the last minute by Count John Capodistrias, the future Governor of Greece, who at that time was serving in the Russian Foreign Ministry.

During military operations carried out between 1809 and 1815 all the Ionian Islands came under the control of Brit-ain. Lefkada was occupied in 1810, and became part of the United State of the Ionian Islands, an autonomous state under British protection (by the Treaty of Paris, 1815). But disputes between the islanders and the British, the Parga tragedy of 1819 and the hostile attitude adopted by the British towards the Greek War of Independence when it broke out in 1821 soon led the islanders to cease obeying their foreign overlords.

On the one hand, for fifty years the islands lived in greater peace and security than they had known for many centuries. Roads, bridges and aqueducts were built, and there was a certain degree of democratic freedom. On the other hand, some of the High Commissioners —notable the first, Sir Thomas Maitland, known as 'King Tom—' behaved with great harshness.

Throughout the 19th century the island was shaken by numerous earthquakes. The worst was that of 1825, which compelled the British to introduce a new anti-seismic building method. This was applied to public buildings, of which the courthouse and the girls' secondary school in I. Tambeliou Square are the only surviving examples.

Under the period of the British 'protectorate' the local people did not have the right to elect their representatives. Initially, only 375 people out of a total population of 17,000 had the right to vote: a number which, just before union with Greece, had risen to 2,135 out of a population of 20,000.

Liberation and After

When the War of Independence against the Turks broke out in 1821, the British did not wish under any circumstances to appear to be helping the Greek rebels. As a result, strict sanctions were applied to any Ionian islanders who tried to send help to mainland Greece. But such British measures proved hard to enforce, and the support of the Ionians turned out to be of great importance for the ultimate success of the struggle for freedom.

The contribution made by Lefkada to the fight for independence of the Greek nation was moral, financial and above all material. Hundreds of experienced fighting men from Lefkada served in the Greek forces, and the island itself was often the scene of military operations.

When Greece won its independence in 1830, the opposition of the Ionian islanders to their foreign conquerors gradually began to grow in strength. However, the British were reluctant to relinquish their sovereignty. When Gladstone visited the islands in 1858, he showered the islanders with promises in the hope that Britain could cling on to control. When he examined the situation on the spot, he declared that to turn the islands over to Greece would be "a crime against European security".

When the Bavarian Othon, first King of Greece, was deposed, the entire country came under British influence. This coincided with a wave of patriotism among the Greeks — particularly the younger generation, those aged between 15 and 24— and led to the incorporation of Lefkada and the other Ionian islands into Greece in 1864.

The middle class or bourgeoisie of Lefkada came into being by the end of the 19th century. It consisted of the townspeople, who grew prosperous at the expense of the villagers, and whose wealth reconciled the old aristocracy to their existence. The working class and the rural population continued —literally and figuratively— to plough their own furrow, a task made more difficult by frequent raids of robber bands from Turkish-occupied Akarnania. The salutations 'sior' and 'effendi' were now heard addressed not only to the former nobility but also to the wealthy members of the middle class. The word 'pro-skyno' —'I bow my head to you— was also used more frequently. However, this interval of prosperity after 1870 came to an end in 1900, when the the island's renowned vineyards were laid waste by a fungus. The solution which emerged was mass emigration to the United States.

Early in this century, Lefkada was one of the most advanced centres in the campaign of liberating the parts of northern Greece which were still oc-

cupied by the Turks. This period was followed by one in which the whole of Greece —and, of course, Lefkada too— was divided into two camps profoundly hostile to one another: the 'monarchist' supporters of King Constantine II —who were in the majority— and the followers of Prime Minister Eleftherios Venizelos. As each party succeeded the other in power, it persecuted those who had won places under the patronage of its predecessor. The difference between the two 'parties' was, in effect, that the monarchists were opposed to Greek entry into the First World War while the Venizelists supported a declaration of war on the side of the Entente.

In 1919, Greece embarked on a campaign to liberate the Greeks of Asia Minor, and Smyrna was occupied by the Greek Army. This was the beginning of a dream — one which turned out to be a nightmare. In 1922, the Army was forced on to the retreat, and the 'Asia Minor catastrophe' brought some 5,000 refugees (of the hundreds of thousands of Greeks who were forced to flee) to a temporary camp inside Santa Maura castle.

Political instability and civil unrest continued until the outbreak of the Second World War.

After 1960, the island began to recover from this hard time, and since 1978 tourism has made a major contribution, bringing new life to the coastal areas. However, this has involved a movement of population from upland villages to Lefkada town and the seaside settlements, as a result of which the pretty upland areas are emptying of their population and the fields now lie fallow. New villages have sprung up along the east coast, and in summer the whole island bustles with life.

A view of the Lefkada channel, with the castle of Santa Maura on the le

d the town in the right background (*Illustrated London News, 1859*).

YESTERDAY AND TODAY

In this attempt to give readers some acquaintance with the personality of Lefkada and its inhabitants, we shall be trying to get as close as possible to the soul of the people; we shall see how they live, their habits and customs, their interests an d their occupations, and everything else which will shed some light upon their character.

Let us begin with the accounts of foreign **travellers** who visited the island after the 18th century. These texts will be followed by other particulars of the past and the present capable of contributing to an undertaking which is ambitious, to say the least.

In 1711, D. Delphin, General Commissioner for the Ionian Islands, wrote a report for the Senate of Venice in which he described the Lefkadans as *"restless and impulsive spirits"*.

Half a century later, Francesco Grimani had this to say of the Lefkadans: *"Their character indicates that they have not yet forgotten the Ottoman yoke. Given that they are only moderately wealthy, they are tolerably quarrelsome; yet they are law-abiding and very obedient whenever the authorities have to intervene. The quality and quantity of their products demonstrate their inclination towards agriculture. Now, the Lefkadans have become law-abiding farmers"*.

In the late 18th century, André Grassel, French Consul in Corfu, wrote that the people of Lefkada were *"upright, peaceful and gullible. They lack vigour, dynamism and ambition, and a small fortune is all they ask"*.

The description left by the French traveller Saint-Souveur is along similar lines: *"They are upright in character, gullible, vigorous and ambitious.*

The accounts left by these travellers sometimes contradict one another — naturally enough, when one remembers that they are personal appreciations. In any case, the differing natures of villagers, townspeople and aristocrats, of seamen and farmers, and — in general — of the behaviour and customs of different people make generalisations impossible, with the exception of those features which life and history have confirmed. Thus, all the travellers remark on the stout-heartedness and bravery of the Lefkadans; this reached its crowning glory in their resistance to having their children carried off by the Turks to be trained as janissaries, and in the large numbers of Lefkadans who fought in the struggle for national liberation.

The **Lefkadans** have the 'island personality', although they also share many features with their neighbours on the mainland — from whom, in any case, there is only a narrow strip of sea to separate them. They are peaceful, vigorous and dynamic people, who are pleased to see visitors and easily open wide the doors to their homes and their hearts. They are ambitious, and can be diabolically cunning when success is at stake.

The **women of Lefkada** attracted the attention of most foreign visitors: Saint-Souveur was particularly impressed by them, and described them as *"generally beautiful and free, with a weakness for jewellery and luxury"*.

The distinctive nature of the women of Lefkada was also, of course, a matter of interest for local authors such as Antonis Tzevelekis, who gives the following picture of how the men of the island saw their womenfolk: *"For us, Woman is a complex form, a distinctive female figure blending austerity and femininity, combining harmony with robustness and sensitivity. The Women of Lefkada are a bridge down the ages for the people of the island, who have known hardship at the hands of God and men alike"*.

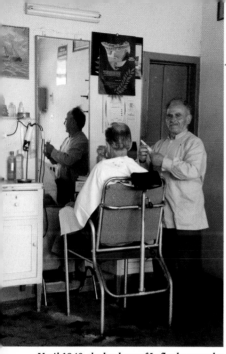

Until 1940, the barbers of Lefkada were the sole producers of the local 'mandolato' and 'pasteli'.

Life and motion in the town of Lefkada focus on the main square and the market area rather than the seafront, as is usual elsewhere. The stone-flagged square is the scene for the continuing tradition of the 'volta', the evening promenade; this custom was so popular amongst Lefkadans of an earlier age that they would go on with their stroll even when it was drizzling, under their umbrellas. Around the square were the old cafes and patisseries, where the strollers would sit to take a break and indulge in a chat. This still goes on today, although most of the traditional cafes have given way to modern cafeterias, patisseries and bars. However, there are still two old-fashioned cafes where 'soumada', the traditional local refreshment, can be enjoyed. The old cafes were frequented chiefly by fishermen and workmen in search of entertainment; they would gather there after the day's toil to sip their Greek coffees or, later in the evening, their carafe of wine. The wind-up gramophone and its records were an essential part of the recreation available in the cafe.

Barbers' shops were another place where the Lefkadans could meet and enjoy themselves. Of course, this traditional role has now gone for ever, but apart from their role in improving the appearance of the male population the barbers' shops are still the only place where high-quality 'mantolato' and 'pasteli', the local confections, can be bought.

The barbers' shops of earlier days enjoyed times of great renown. Furnished with outstanding taste, they would have engravings or lithographs of historical events, romantic scenes or tableaux from operas. From the ceiling would hang cages of songbirds — canaries, finches, linnets— which the barbers themselves caught with bird-lime. The barbers of Lefkada were restless souls by nature, fond of reading, of intelligent conversation, of the typical jokes and pranks of the island. They usually spoke Italian and invariably played one musical instrument or another. Every barber's shop had its instrument, often a mandolin, to the accompaniment of which the local 'cantades' or even extracts from operas would be sung. Apart from their own profession, the barbers were often eminent in other areas — such as medicine, where they kept up the tradition common in pre-scientific societies.

A Lefkadan woman in traditional dress. In the background, the town of Lefkada.

Brotherhood and joy at the Festival of Language and the Arts

The Lefkadan tradition —and much of the island's character— was on display at the **religious feasts** and **holidays** celebrated in each of the villages, where old **ccustoms** were revived each year and handed down from generation to generation. All the saints' days commemorated on Lefkada were accompanied by feasts — and that meant dancing, singing and the consumption of large quantities of food and wine. In the villages, it was the custom for treats to be sent to the group of dancers performing at any time: these would take the form of ouzo, beer or wine for the men, and Turkish delight or trinkets for the women. The best-known of the island feast days are those of Our Lady 'Faneromeni' in the town itself, of St Kyriaki at Nidri.

The most important non-religious event on Lefkada is the annual Festival of *Language and the Arts*, which has been held each summer for the last thirty years and which has been equally successful each time. During the Festival there is an influx of visitors into Lefkada: the events have widespread appeal for both Greeks and foreign visitors.

The first ten days of the Festival are devoted to 'language' in the general sense: speeches, discussions, conferences and symposia, together with theatrical performances. Over the years, scores of leading figures in the modern intellectual and artistic world —including the famous Greek soprano Maria Callas— have appeared at the Festival.

The second ten-day period is given up to folklore. Dance teams from all over the world take part in the International Festival of Folk Dance. Bonds of friendship are created at the Festival which often lead to the same teams coming back year and year again. The borders go down between Greece and neighbours such as Bulgaria and Yugoslavia, as well as with more distant countries such as Russia, Israel and even Senegal, and the folk performers join with the Lefkadans in furthering the brotherhood of man in every possible way. The Festival makes Lefkada a place where peoples of all races and colours can meet in equal fraternity.

The **major feast days of the Orthodox Church** are celebrated in a manner typical of the island. At dawn on *New Year's Day*, the traditional 'diana' takes place on the streets of the town. Islanders old and young —after spending New Year's Eve playing the card games which, according to custom, ensure good luck in the coming year— gather in the main square beneath the Town Band building. As the Band emerges, playing the 'dawn march', the entire crowd follows, throwing vegetables at each other, pushing, shoving and indulging in horseplay which is never taken amiss. Fishing-boats are hauled up into the square; cans, barrels and anything else capable of making a deafening noise are rolled around the square and through the streets — indeed, it has been known for entire kiosks to shift site on this occasion! In earlier times, when the water supply still came through standpipes and fountains, the women would go out at this time to bring home the 'silent water', which they had to carry home without speaking, even if someone broke their jug. The water was sprinkled throughout the house and all the members of the family drank some: this was believed to bring good luck.

At *Christmas* and at *New Year,* visitors to the house would be offered the traditional New Year cake or 'kourmades'. In earlier times, the women of Lefkada —especially in the villages— knew very little about the art of baking confectionaries. Those who were fond of sweet things were thought of as soft and prodigal. As a result, the same cake —with minor variations— was made for weddings and funerals. 'Kourmades' are the honey-cakes known elsewhere in Greece as 'melomakarona'.

On the feast of *Epiphany*, the whole town gathers on the sea-front for the ceremony of the blessing of the waters. As the priest throws the cross into the water, according to the ritual, the islanders dip branches laden with oranges into the sea: one of these is later placed among the icons in the corner shrine, and the rest are eaten.

The *Carnival period* on Lefkada is also full of traditions. In former times there were processions with decorated floats and feasting in the streets and squares, not to mention the balls organised by the aristocracy in their clubs and in the restaurants. Even today, the island's associations and societies hold dances in richly decorated halls. The Carnival closes with a parade and with a maypole erected in the main square: on the last Sunday in Carnival, before the first day of Lent, this is burned.

Easter is celebrated on Lefkada in an atmosphere of great religious devotion. In earlier times, the priests used to re-enact the Last Supper on Maundy Thursday, following the description given in the Gospels, on a platform outside the church of St Spyridon. On Good Friday, after the Descent from the Cross, the girls dressed the catafalques with flowers and there was serious competition as to which church would have the most beautifully decorated. The custom of the Good Friday processions starting out simultaneously from each church on Easter Eve and converging on the main square went back to Venetian times. When the processions met, each part of the town had its own signal cry: that of St Haralambos was ''main sheet away!'', from the large population of sailors, and that of St Demetrius was *'shrimps - shrimps'* because most of the people who lived there were fishermen. Nowadays, the procession with the catafalque takes place on the evening of Good Friday. The processions continue to meet in the square, where a short service is held to the accompaniment of the Town Band and the local choirs. The Band is out on the streets again on Easter

Eve morning, playing merry tunes; the church bells ring, and the housewives throw unwanted pieces of earthenware and crockery out of the windows as a symbol of 'revenge' on the Jews who crucified Christ. *'There goes another one'*, they say as they do so. After the service on Easter Eve, the custom is to eat tripe rather than the special Easter soup ('mageiritsa') consumed elsewhere in Greece. On the evening of Easter Sunday there used to be a special *'Resurrection litany'* and icons from all the churches were borne in procession round the town. The processions met, once more, in the square, and a firework display was held. This custom has now died out. Mid-day on Easter Sunday is the time when family groups get together to eat and drink, but the spit-roasting of whole lambs —done elsewhere in Greece on Sunday— continues to be a feature of Easter Monday in Lefkada.

The two most important religious festivals: the Litany of Our Lady 'Faneromeni' and the Good Friday procession.

Weddings were events of great importance in the life of the islanders, and they were associated with great ritual in the period of preparation, during the wedding itself and in its aftermath. Today, of course, the current of 'modernisation' and levelling down means that weddings are not celebrated as they were in the past, and many of the customs are dying out. However, on 11 August the traditional island wedding is revived in all its intricacy and splendour in the village of Karya.

After the work of the matchmaker —who might be male or female— had been completed, the *draft dowry agreement* was taken to the bridegroom's house and read out. If the bridegroom found it satisfactory, he would wish the agreement 'good fortune' and a party would begin, lasting all night. In the morning, when the bride's relatives left, they would take with them the confections and other treats provided by the future in-laws. These were placed in a kerchief which the bridegroom had bought for the bride. On the following Sunday, the bridegroom's father visited the bride's family, bearing the ring, and the exact date on which the engagement ceremony would take place was arranged.

The engagement ceremony was also called the *'simadouria'*, or *'marking ceremony'*, since the gold jewellery given to the bride was supposed to leave its mark on her. The most common kinds of jewellery given at this time were rings, ear-rings (of various types), pins and brooches. All the gifts were put into a finely-woven basket covered with a coloured kerchief (usually red). A girl (both of whose parents had to be alive) then carried the basket to the bride's house on her head. The date of the wedding was set later, and as the time approached, the bride's preparations became more and more

intense. Among her chief tasks was making ready the wool with which mattresses, pillows and bolsters would be stuffed.

On the Tuesday and Wednesday of the week before the wedding, the special bread for the bridegroom and the bride, respectively, was kneaded. On the Thursday, a woman was asked to the bride's house to fill and sew up the mattresses, the pillows and the bolsters. On the Friday evening, the bride's trousseau —in which each individual item of clothing was marked with a stitch of red thread— was counted, and the bundles in which the dowry would be transported were moved. The official invitations to the wedding were made on the Saturday morning. Two or three men whose job this was went from house to house inviting everyone to attend. In their hands they held bags filled with treats from the in-laws (rusks, almond sweets, walnuts, and so on). As the sun set, the *'fatted calf'* (in this case, a two or three year-old billy goat) would be slaughtered. It was generally regarded as a duty in the village that all the streets and courtyards through which the wedding procession would pass should be carefully swept and freshly white-washed.

On the Sunday morning, the bride's 'dresser' was about her business at an early hour. It was far from easy to dress the bride, particularly when she was to wear the 'Romaika' costume of Lefkada, with its thousand and one details. As the bride was dressing, so, too, was the bridegroom, so as to be ready for the great moment. The bride went to church on horseback; the wedding service followed, and then a feast with singing and dancing to violins and the local variation of the lute. On the Monday morning, the 'well ceremony' was held: the bride's in-laws went with her to the well or the foun-

A local folk dance, from the Festival of Language and the Arts.

tain, taking the shift she had worn on her wedding night, known as the 'banner of her honour as a bride'. On their return, the women made a kind of pie with flour, olive oil, sugar or honey, and before the sun set the dough was rolled out.

On the first Sunday after the wedding, bride and bridegroom went to church. After the service, one of the churchwardens presented them with the *'fiora'*, a tray containing pretty bouquets of local flowers. When church was over, the bridge and groom went back to the bride's house, her first visit home since the wedding.

Folk music continues to play an important part in life on Lefkada. Today, as in the past, the mouthorgan, the guitar, the mandolin and the accordion spring to life in the hands of the local people. A pronounced influence from the mainland —due to

the island's proximity to Akarnania—is obvious, and there are also Western influences, particularly those of Italy, which can be seen in the 'cantades', the frequent singing of opera areas, and the 'korones'. The Town Band —the oldest in Greece, founded in 1850— was a truly daring undertaking for poverty-stricken Lefkada, given its financial plight and the political circumstances of the time. However, it was a reflection of the progressive mentality of the islanders and their fondness for culture; they realised that in music they lagged behind what they had already achieved in the theatre. Even today, choirs, mandolin groups, bands and children's bands are only too willing to appear on the streets and in the squares whenever there is an anniversary or some other festival — and there are more than a few of these during the course of the year.

The **dances of Lefkada** are an in-separable part of the island's tradition. There is a clear influence from Roumeli, or southern central Greece, transmitted from the nearby mainland. The *Milia* or *Militsa* ('apple tree') dance is a mixture of the cross-wise and circular pattern of steps, while *Yannos o Marathianos* or *Peratianos* has steps from the mainland 'syrtos' and 'tsamikos' dances. The *Theiakos* is another dance reminiscent of the 'syrtos'. The *'syrtos'* itself is danced on the island, as are the Kalamatianos and *tsamikos* dances performed throughout Greece. Those who are fortunate enough to attend one of the many local festivals and feasts will be able to see these dances performed, and will have an opportunity to admire the manliness o f the male dancers and the elegance of the women. In addition, they will have a chance to see the traditional Lefkadan costumes, which are of exceptional interest.

The Lefkada Band is the oldest in Greece.

Lokal island costumes

The French traveller Saint Souveur has left us the following description of the **female costume of Lefkada**: *"Their costume, like that of the men, is Oriental. The women do whatever they can to make it look more ornamental. All the dresses are embroidered with gold, silver or silk. Even the shifts and long, wide petticoats worn under their skirts are richly embroidered. The wedding dress is made of white silk, embroidered with gold along the hem and at the throat."*

The female costume consists of a skirt with many pleats. The *'kotolo'* is worn beneath it, the *'spaletta'* adorns the bosom and a kerchief covers the head. In the winter, the women put a cape across their shoulders, while the girls wear shawls and old women keep themselves warm beneath a rug. The *'spaletta'* is decorated with brooches and pins, while a c ross is worn round the throat and ear-rings are common.

The Lefkadans were the last of the Ionian islanders to be faithful to their traditional costume. Rather than trousers, the men wore the *'bourzana'* with embroidery on the shins, an embroidered shirt with broad sleeves and a brocade waistcoat. They preferred the *'kamze'*, a short-sleeved coat, to the jacket. Around the waist they would wear a knitted belt with a width of 20 cm and a length of 2 metres. Headgear consisted of a kerchief or the *'skortzes'*, a cap with a tassel. Clogs were worn with gaiters.

The bridal costume —notable for its elegance, grace and nobility— was particularly impressive. Here there was a clear influence from the Aegean islands, although the Italian elements were also prominent. This costume was initially the festive garb of the more prosperous inhabitants of Lefkada town.

The first item of bridal dress was the

dress: this was made of rather thick silk, in delicate, subtle shades of red, green or blue. It reached down to the ground, and was broad and heavily-pleated beneath the waist. On the bosom, the opening where the dress buttoned was covered by a large kerchief in a light colour, the *'paleta'*, to which the bride's gold jewellery would be pinned.

Across her shoul-ders she would wear the *'tzoubes'*, a kind of coat with short sleeves and padded shoulders. Her head would be covered with a white kerchief reaching far down her back; printed and embroidered, this was known as the *'kefalopani'*. Beneath it was a small black fez embroidered with silk, silver and gold. Of particular elegance was the *'tremou-la'*, a small gold crest on top of the fez whose topmost plume was adorned with pearls. The back and sleeves of the *'tzoubes'* were also finely embroidered, and pearl ear-rings were worn. The bride would wear white gloves and stockings, while in order to make her look plumper three 'kotola' were worn around the waist. Two of these were coloured, and the outermost was white cambric decorated with lace.

This marvellous bridal costume can be seen at the old village of Karya during the revival of the traditional village wedding held there every year on 11 August.

In the main square of Karya, under the plane trees and by the fountains, one can still see today the lissom girls of the village carrying vast pots of water on their heads. The secret of how these huge weights are carried with such apparent ease belongs only to the village women of Lefkada.

The local women can be reminiscent of the Caryatides on the Acropolis at Athens.

Marriage is not only an important landmark in the life of each individual; it is also a symbol of the continuity of life, of the future of the village. The little community will acquire one more household — a household whose interior would, in the past, have resembled the graphic description given in his poem 'Photeinos' by the great Lefkadan poet Aristotelis Valaoritis:

And hundreds of bits and bobs scattered about here and there,
a riddle, a baking-board, a rolling-pin
and a spinning-wheel with
the threads, the distaff and the bobbin,
the box with the multi-coloured balls
of wool,
and a hanging basket of pastry near
the chimney,

and a lamp in the corner with the
salt-cellar,
and the poor man's cooking-pots
and the farmer's implements, whips
and reaping-hooks,
and a pile of forks, and a bunch of
olive poles,
and two untouched baskets of seeds
sent with two ploughs
to the ploughman, by his friends,
when they heard about the unexpected
misfortune
which had overtaken him.

The position in which each village was built was influenced by the tendency for life on the island to gravitate towards its interior, for reasons of safety.

As a rule, villages were built away from the sea and in such a position as

The loom and the oven were essential parts of ev

to be invisible from it. They might be placed in ravines (as were Alatro and Haradiatika), behind hills (like Englouvi) or in dense woods (Syvros and Vournikas).

This, then, was the main factor in choosing the site for the village, but there were also others, such as the availability of water, the suitability of the soil, the direction in which it would face, and shelter from the wind. Villages which had no natural protection against pirate raids, such as Mara-ntochori, were built on the steepest part of their sites so that they could be defended, and the houses were given some of the features of fortifications (e.g. embrasures for rifles, cellars without windows, turrets, etc.).

In general, the villages in the south of ousehold.

Traditional island architecture.

Lefkada, which are close to the plain of Vasiliki, whose abundant water is a source of life, have preserved in their architecture some traces of prosperity — prosperity which was, however, confined to the houses of the large landowners. These houses still give such villages an air of gentility, while the character of the villages of northern Lefkada was defined by the 'ordinary' people who lived there. Their level of economic development was never more than tolerable.

The mountainous parts of the island and their vegetation guaranteed the local people the three materials most basic for building: wood, stone and water. Clay was little used, though there were clay-pits in the Ayios Petros area (Marathias) and kilns operated there producing pottery and other such things.

The **architecture** of Lefkada, like that of the other Ionian Islands, was influenced by the West. However, the local tradition continued to be relatively strong, thanks to the proximity of mainland Greece.

It would be an omission not to refer to the watermills (at Haradiatika) and windmills (at Yira and Sfakiotes) which have fallen into disuse after being supplanted by diesel-powered milling machinery. Roofless and ruinous today, they are visited only by birds and snakes.

The island and its surrounding area are quite often shaken by earthquakes. The Lefkadans have had to learn to live with seismic activity and have lost their fear of it. This has had an impact on the island's architecture: the houses are now built so as to resist earthquakes. The houses are often built close together —in the medieval fashion— as a rule without gardens and with only small courtyards crammed with geraniums and pots of basil. Initially, most of the houses had two storeys, of which the ground floor was stone-built and the upper structure wooden; this was often timbered on the outside, too. Some such houses have survived, with their external timbering blackened now and cracked. Later, a third storey was added, and glassed-in balconies became common. Together with the colonnades down the sides of the street, these were essential on an island where rain is frequent.

There were also, of course, what were described by the locals as 'mansions', the dwellings of the landowners. Architecturally, these differed little from ordinary houses, but they were more richly decorated inside, were higher and had wooden ceilings. In general, more care and attention was lavished on them.

Even today —just to be on the safe side— many people still build wood-framed houses, which contrast sharply with the standard Modern Greek reinforced concrete structures. These houses will be found along the maze of narrow cobbled alleyways which branch off each other throughout the town and lead to the main square. In many places, the original cobbles have now been replaced with cement. The purpose of the labyrinthine arrangement of streets was to disorient raiding pirates, while at the same time keeping the neighbourhoods snug against the cold winter winds. Even today, the 'kantounia', as they are known, fill with housewives sitting on stools at the gates of their whitewashed courtyards. This is the way to make the most of warm winter afternoons or cool summer evenings; coffee is drunk and local affairs are debated as the women knit or sew, while all around the shouts of children at play echo from the alley walls.

In matters of religion, the Venetians were much more tolerant towards the Lefkadans than the Turks. Not only were the islanders allowed complete freedom in performing their religious duties, but they were even facilitated in the building of churches. As a result, a wave of religious fervour swept the island in the 17th century: large numbers of churches were built in the town and the countryside, the monasteries were at their most prosperous and icon-painting flourished.

Unfortunately, the earthquake of November 1948 did a great deal of damage to the churches of Lefkada, and particularly to those in the town itself. Yet an even greater menace has stemmed from subsequent neglect — although given that most of the churches are privately-owned, perhaps some proprietors can be excused on the grounds of impecuniousness.

The town **churches** are the only buildings to be constructed entirely in stone. Since, as noted above, most are privately-owned, it is not always easy to visit them.

The Byzantine style of church-building must certainly have been implemented in Lefkada, but it was soon abandoned because of the difficulties involved in rebuilding after each earthquake. The much simpler form of the single-aisled wooden-roofed basilica was adopted instead. For even great safety, a wooden frame was usually installed along the inner side of the walls, so as to prevent the structure from collapsing inwards and protect the congregation in the event of an earthquake.

Almost all the churches in Lefkada are single-aisled rectangular basilicas with a semi-circular arch. The roofs are tiled and divided into two vaults, while there is usually a wooden ceiling inside. The churches which date back to Turkish times are further out in the countryside and often small, simple structures without any attempt to decorate the facade. Such churches were also erected in the Venetian period, but only when they had to be built quickly to deal with some religious need. The only external decoration, found in a very small number of churches, consists of faience plates embedded in the walls.

The relatively large churches we see in the town today were also small and constructed in this manner when first built. This can be verified from the applications from local residents kept in the local Archives (one of only two such rich collections in Greece) seeking permission from the Venetian authorities to build "a small church" in one place or another. These first churches had a strong whiff of the mainland about them, since the masons were usually from the mountains of Epirus.

A stone relief in the form of a face above a door in Lefkada.

Damage by earthquakes caused the frequent rebuilding or renovation of these churches. The form of church constructed at a later date was the result of the powerful influence of the churches of Zakynthos, in conjunction with the economic and cultural progress of the island in the 18th century. Indeed, as the course of history turned out, the churches of Lefkada outlived their originals and are of the greatest value now: their models on Zakynthos were flattened in the earthquake of 1953.

The carefully-constructed doors of the churches have carved lintels and capitals. Their door-posts are flanked by protruding pillars with capitals which support the lintel. The windows are miniature versions of the doors, and are decorated in the same manner. On the west facade, above the door, there is almost always a Gothic rosette.

The bell-tower of St Minas and Our Lady 'Vrysiotissa'

The question of whether or not to include a bell-tower was not one which seriously engaged the interest of builders, down to the early 19th century at least. In the case of the small countryside churches, the bell-tower was built on as an extension to one wall of the church, rising, after the early Venetian period, in the form of an arch. The repeated flattening of these bell-towers by earthquake action made such structures both dangerous and expensive when they were of any height. For that reason, the second decade of the 20th century saw the introduction —especially in Lefkada town— *of iron belfries in the shape of towers, many of which had clocks as well as bells.*

Until the 17th c., wall-paintings were the only form of decoration used in churches. Most of the paintings to have survived —usually in country churches— date from the 18th c., although those in Our Lady Hodeghetria outside the town are 15th c. work. It would seem that in these early days there were no local icon-painters, and the only name to have come down to us is that of Fotis Kolyvas (1761), who was from Preveza on the mainland. From the stylistic point of view, some of the wall-paintings are reminiscent of Zakynthos and some of mainland Greece, while Western influences can be seen in a third group.

By way of contrast with the literary sphere, the period of Venetian rule was notable for the number of craftsmen who lived or worked on the island. These icon-painters, wood-carvers and goldsmiths produced works of art of lasting value and interest.

Artistic production in Lefkada was always directly related to religious needs, and not with demand from society. Churches were a focus for artistic as well as religious life. Liberation from the Turkish yoke caused enthusiasm which was expressed in religious feasts, and above all in the rebuilding and decoration of churches, many of which became fascinating monuments.

St Minas

The following Lefkadan 'tagiadori' (wood-carvers) were well known in the late 19th century: **Panos Prosalentis** or **Maistralis** (1822-1894), works by whom can be seen in the church of St Demetrius in the town. His sons **Efstathios** and **Dionysios Prosalentis** carried on the family tradition: among the work of the former (1856-1922) is the screen in Our Lady of the Strangers, the pulpit in Our Lady the Bringer of Good News and, outside the town, the bishop's throne and the screen in the Faneromeni Monastery. **Dionysios Prosalentis** (? - 1940) produced the screens for the churches of St Stephen in Exantheia and St Demetrius at Drymonas. Among the more recent practitioners of the art was **Yannis Vretos** (1871-1969), a pupil of Panos Prosalentis and an artist influenced by Efstathios Prosalentis, who carved the screens for a large number of churches on the island.

Painting, too, was closely bound up with the depiction of religious scenes in churches, and was also subject to the fact that painters were forced to turn their hand to what came their way in order to make a living. In the work of the few early Lefkadan painters we will find no landscapes or other secular scenes: apart from icons, they also produced portraits, but only when specially commissioned to do so.

Among the better-known painters of the 18th and 19th centuries were **Ioannis Roussos** (17 79-1851), **Spyridon Vendouras** (1761-1835), **Spyridon Gazis** (1835-1890), **Vasileios Sideris** (1856-1907) and **Leonidas Sideris** (1870-1957). The painters **Panayiotis** and **Nikolaos Doxaras** (late 17th century) of Zakynthos, **Tomaso Gen** (1700-1755), **Konstantinos Kontarinis** (early 18th century) and **N. Koutouzis** (late 18th century) also worked on the island. Works by all

A work by Ioannis Roussos from the Museum of Post-Byzantine Art.

these painters can be seen in the island's churches and the town museum.

Today, there are quite a number of painters on the island and numerous Lefkadan artists work in other parts of Greece. Naturally enough, there are many amateur painters, too.

Among the best-known Lefkadan artists are **K. Glenis, Sideris Panagos, K. Katopodis** and **I. Konidaris.** The well-known art teacher **Theodoros Stamos** is a Lefkadan, and spends much of his time living and working on the island.

By way of contrast to the other Ionian islands —Corfu and Zakynthos in particular— the long period of Venetian rule made little impression on the **dialect** of Lefkada.

However, the lack of schools and indeed of education in any form whatever meant that the island made no significant contribution to **literature.** Thus, we cannot really speak of Lefkadan literature in the Venetian period. However, the fact that the Venetian state was well organised and administered meant that some of the islanders did gain academic training, becoming lawyers, notaries, pharmacists and doctors. After their studies at Italian universities, they brought back with them literary texts which were widely read and discussed in the island's salons. Gradually, the first timid shoots of local intellectual production began to sprout.

The intellectual atmosphere in the town of Lefkada became a little more intense; the thoughts of all were guided first by the great goal of national liberation and later by the desire for the unification of the Ionian islands with what was now the free Greek state. By the mid-19th century, the island's few literary figures - headed by Aristotelis Valaoritis (1824-1879) took the nation's struggle for freedom as the central theme in their texts.

Among earlier writers were Ioannis Stamatelos (1822-1881), Dimitrios Petritsopoulos (1763-1833), Ioannis Zambelios (1787-1856), an author of historical dramas, and Athanasios Politis (1796-1864).

Spyridon Zambelios (1813-1881), who made a name for himself in Greek letters more generally, was the son of Ioannis Zambelios. After beginning his education on Lefkada, he later studied abroad. Zambelios was the first modern Greek historian to grasp the importance of the continuity of the Greek nation from antiquity down to the present day. Spyridon Zambelios is widely regarded as one of Greece's earliest and most important historians, and he founded Byzantine studies as we know them today. His literary work *Cretan Wedding* (1871) is among the most representative Greek literary texts of the 19th century.

It is, perhaps, interesting that of the great Greek 'national' poets, three — Dionysios Solomos, Angelos Sikelianos and Aristotelis Valaoritis— were from the Ionian Islands, and the latter two were Lefkadans.

Aristotelis Valaoritis (1824-1879) was a patriotic poet and politician. His family originated on the mainland, and distinguished itself in the struggle for independence from the Turks.

Valaoritis himself spent his youth studying abroad, marrying in 1852 and then returning home. Once back in Lefkada, he threw himself into politics: he was a member of the Ionian Assembly and, after the union, of the Greek Parliament.

He was a distinguished public speaker. For some years, his political activities overshadowed his poetry, which is profoundly patriotic: he sings the praises of the rugged mountain people who fought the Turks, and he narrates incidents from recent Greek history.

Valaoritis' house, on the islet of Madouri in Nidri bay, still stands but is in private ownership and not open to the public.

I. Zambelios, member of the Society of Friends.

The poet Aristotelis Valaoritis.

Angelos Sikelianos (1884-1951) is one of the greatest poets of modern Greece and an important figure in European literature. Sikelianos' vision of a revival of the ancient Greek spirit permeates the greater part of his poetry, which is consciously exhortatory, optimistic and enthusiastic. The same theme lay behind what as widely seen as his life's work: the revival of the Delphi Festival.

After 1927, Sikelianos and his American wife Eva used the theatre at Delphi for performances of the ancient drama, dance and music. These productions, which attracted worldwide interest, breathed fresh life into the stagnant atmosphere which dominated the approach to ancient Greek culture in the inter-War period, and their impact can still be felt even today. Nonetheless, the Delphi Festi-

val was treated with complete indifference by the state and Sikelianos' vision never came to fruition.

Sikelianos' progressive ideas also barred him from the Nobel Prize, despite his being proposed twice by a host of eminent foreign literary figures. For the same reason, he never became a member of the Athens Academy.

Lafcadio Hearn (1850-1904) was perhaps the most unusual of the three cases. He was born in Lefkada to a British father who was an army doctor and a mother from Kythera, who may have been of Maltese extraction. Although he left Lefkada at an early age, he took it with him wherever he went — not least in his name. After studying in Ireland and England, he went to America in 1869, where he worked as

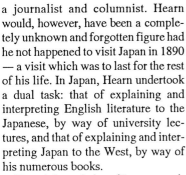

Angelos Sikelianos

Lafcadio Hearn (Yakomo Kuizumi)

a journalist and columnist. Hearn would, however, have been a completely unknown and forgotten figure had he not happened to visit Japan in 1890 — a visit which was to last for the rest of his life. In Japan, Hearn undertook a dual task: that of explaining and interpreting English literature to the Japanese, by way of university lectures, and that of explaining and interpreting Japan to the West, by way of his numerous books.

Hearn's knowledge of Japanese culture was such that he won the respect even of Japanese scholars. In recent years, his renown has brought many Japanese visitors to Lefkada.

The **theatre** in Lefkada developed in a manner comparable to that of literature in general. In the early 19th century, small companies (usually of amateurs) organised performances on the occasion of special feast-days or receptions.

Around 1848 the first foreign companies were invited to the island, from Italy.

In about 1850 the Daston family founded Lefkada's first theatre, and 1856 saw the *formation of the Dramatic Society*, whose purpose was to sponsor theatrical performances and also encourage those who were in a position to write or translate plays. Local amateur theatrical associations were set up by young men and women of good birth.

This was the first time such initiatives had been taken anywhere in Greece, and they created a strong impression both on the island and elsewhere.

The Lefkadans are an industrious people, and they managed to make the barren soil of their island fruitful and profitable by the sweat of their brows, leaving not one single patch of earth untilled. Their patience, perseverence and love of their native soil hewed fields out of the bare rock; with the primitive tools at their disposal, they hacked fields out of the mountainsides and built terraces like huge flights of steps, supported by drystone retaining walls constructed with the stones removed from the fields.

There, they grew —and grow today— grapes, olives and the other products essential for their diet: mostly beans of various sorts.

The terraces can still be seen particularly clearly on the hillsides around the villages of Exanthia, Sfakiotes, Karya, Englouvi, Hortata, Drymonas and Kalamitsi. In the past, however, the short and rather bushy Lefkadan vines were more productive than they are today, and wine was made more systematically.

A typical mountain landscape.

The variety of grape grown was usually that locally called *'vartsami'*, which was presumably imported by the Venetians, since a variety called *'barzamino'* is still grown around Venice today. The red wine of the vartsami grapes was usually bought up by French and Italian growers, as fortification for their own wines.

The United Company, the Wine-Making Company, the Wine and Alcohol Company and TAOL (the Wine-Producers' Protection Fund of Lefkada — still in operation today) harvested the grapes from all over the island and processed them. Among the kinds of wine produced were 'keropati', 'yomatari', white Muscat and 'lagero'. This wine, whether bottled or draught (in barrels), was sold either through the co-operatives or in tavernas; in the latter case, it was stored in huge barrels whose presence all around the room was one of the most characteristic features of the old Lefkadan taverna. Today, however, very little wine is still made, and as a consequence barrel-making has almost died out, too. Conditions have changed, and have been responsible for compelling many villagers to take the road of emigration from the island.

Something similar happened with the production of olive oil. The hundreds of thousands of silver-green olive trees all over the island, many of them enormous and centuries old, casting deep shadow in the most unexpected places and running down as far as the sea-shore where only tamarisks normally grow, are evidence that the production of olive oil is one of the oldest occupations of the Lefkadans.

Olive oil was an affair which involved the entire family. When the harvest season came around, men and women would head down to the olive groves.

The process of shaking the fruit down from the trees was fatiguing and sometimes dangerous, and so blankets or tarpaulins were often spread beneath the tree to catch the fruit as it fell naturally. Since about 1965, nets have been used for this purpose. After harvesting, the olives were taken to the press, made into oil and stored in 'kades', huge wooden vats kept in the basements of the houses.

Another important crop was lentils, which were sown in January and harvested in August. The choicest lentils were those of Englouvi, which were cultivated in large fields on the Ayios Donatos plateau, which had been used for this purpose for centuries. On 7 August each year, an old custom is revived up on the plateau: Greek lentil soup is boiled up in a huge cauldron and all those who attend the ceremony receive a plateful, accompanied by olives, bread and salt sardines.

The Englouvi plateau, at a height of 950 metres, has another interesting feature: the vaulted stone structures like large open-air ovens, some 150 in number, which stand scattered here and there. These are known as 'volta', and they were used as temporary shelters for crops, animals or even people. The area of the plateau has been used most cleverly, and the slope of the ground exploited skilfully in arranging the fields which, together with the frequent threshing-floors, create levels which shift and interchange pleasantly.

There were two salt-pans on Lefkada, both to the south of the town. The lower (Kato) salt-pan has not been used since before the War, while the upper (Pano) pan still produces salt today. In the past, the salt was gathered by women who came down from the villages to work for near-starvation wages and in very difficult conditions. The baskets they had to lift often weighed more than half a hundredweight. While gathering the salt, the women also picked tamarisks.

With the passage of time, the only crop which has managed to survive to any extent on the island is the olive, which is cultivated almost exclusively for olive oil. Vines are grown now only in the mountains and foothills of the west of the island; the wine produced is exported to be used as colouring in other varieties of wine. Beekeeping has grown, however: the vegetation which is indigenous to Lefkada is naturally rich in nectar, and so the honey produced is of the highest quality. Beekeeping has now developed into something of a local tradition. Apart from this, the occupational concerns of the islanders are fish-farming, fishing, small-scale craft industry, handicrafts and, of course, tourism.

The island contin

After crossing the bridge across the Lefkada Channel we pass between two fish-farms, the Large (Megalo) and Small (Mikro) Avlemonas, which supply the markets of the island itself and the mainland. This fish is usually served boiled with olive oil and lemon dressing or marinaded ('savoro') by the tavernas of Lefkada, and it makes an excellent accompaniment to the local wine.

Air-dried salami, the confections called 'mandolata' and 'pasteli' and 'village-style' biscuits are among the products turned out by the local cottage industries.

Tourism is still very much a family affair and has not become an impersonal cosmopolitan business activity. By comparison with the other islands, it came very late to Lefkada, and it has not affected the nature or psychology of the islanders, who strive to keep alive as much as they can of their traditions.

fishing tradition in deep waters and also in the shallows of the lagoon.

Detail of a Lefkadan embroidery (17th-18th century).

There are many centuries of tradition behind the contribution which women make to the island's cottage industries. Among the most famous local figures was Maria Stavraka (fl. c. 1900), whose woven goods and embroideries were prized far beyond the island and even outside the frontiers of Greece.

The Nikolis, Manesi and Ayios Petros woven goods produced on the looms in those villages travel all over the world; the women of Lefkada have the secret of fine work and warm colours, creations in which tradition is bound up with functionality and homeliness.

Some of the works produced on the looms of Lefkada —'apladia', 'badanies' and carpets unique for their design and colour— are real museum pieces. There is a large selection in one of the shops in the market, and more —together with a host of other folk culture items— can be seen in the Orpheus Museum of Folk Art. At Karya, the women bring incredible patience to bear on the embroidery done in the local stitch, and this can also be seen in a permanent exhibition in the main street. The traditional style of embroidery (as practiced in the town itself, in the Sfakiotes area, in Karya and in Karyotes) cannot be produced mechanically, and only the island's seamstresses, with their needles and multicoloured threads, can continue to record on cloth their impressions of humans, animals and nature.

The women of Lefkada are as industrious as the men, and there is work for them to do across the whole range of family activities: housework, baking, grinding flour, picing the grapes and olives, digging in the fields. *And if the woman of Lefkada is a queen within her household, then the loom at which she spends much of her time is her throne.* These swift-fingered, elegant women bring to the linen on which they embroider all the wealth of their aesthetic criteria, their deep-rooted spontaneity and their infallible popular taste as they work the shuttle in and out of the red, yellow and azure threads. The Lefkadan women are the guardians of the island's traditions: they preserve its customs, implanting their heritage into the receptive minds of the younger generation and bringing particular care, consistency and affection to organising the life of the island.

This chapter, with its references to the past and the present, may have brought readers closer to the island's life and its people. However, a tour of Lefkada is sure to reveal much more than a mere text can ever hope to convey.

Lefkadan women bring all their sensitivity to bear on their renowned embroidery and weaving.

54

A TOUR OF THE ISLAND

Our tour begins in Lefkada town, which, with its castle, is the first place we come to as we approach the island.

Since some visitors may want to move straight on to other parts of the island, this is perhaps the right place for some instructions.

There are two main roads south from Lefkada town, joining at Vasiliki and forming a circular route round the island. One of these goes down the east coast, passing through Nidri before reaching **Vasiliki,** while the other travels the length of the north western coast before ending at the same destination or Cape Lefkatas. To take either of these roads, we turn left after crossing the causeway and reaching the town and head along the sea-front. This wide road soon turns away

A panoramic view of the Lefk

from the sea, leading to a crossroads at which we turn left (there is no sign-post, but the church on the right is a good landmark). Immediately after this is a fork, at which we bear left. Before long we come to another fork, signposted left for Karya, Nidri and Vasiliki. Those who wish to drive down the north west coast head right here, while the road straight ahead goes to Nidri and Vasiliki.

Visitors who wish to go straight to Ayios Nikitas will turn right at the end of the causeway with its humped bridge over the channel. This road (Angelou Sikelianou Ave.) runs along beside the lagoon. At the new court-house we bear left, and then right (signpost) for Ayios Nikitas.

Those who wish to visit the town first would do well to park somewhere near the harbour: the main street of Lefkada is narrow and parking is not allowed.

nnel and the medieval castle.

The Town of Lefkada

To town of Lefkada is on the north eastern corner of the island, very close to the mainland, to which it is linked by a causeway crossing the Lefkada channel and bordering on the lagoon. We shall be dealing in more detail later with the history of this causeway and of the castle which stands on it.

The town of Lefkada does not have the Venetian atmosphere of Corfu or the elegance which can be discerned in the restored town of Zakynthos. There are a number of historical reasons for this.

First of all, as we have seen in the chapter on the island's history, Venetian rule did not last long enough to leave indelible traces on Lefkada. Second, such Venetian government as there was concentrated on the castle and paid no particular attention to the town. In any case, there was very little building on the site occupied by the town until into the 18th century: the town and the castle were one and the same thing. Third —and most important— is the fact that Lefkada never enjoyed the prosperity of Zakynthos or Corfu.

After the earthquake of 1948, and particularly after 1971, the town began to spread westwards, into a district formerly occupied by dense olive groves. According to the most recent census (1991), the permanent population of the town is 6,700. However, a figure of around 8,000 would probably be more accurate.

Another factor which should not be overlooked, in order to gain a realistic picture of the situation, is that until recently the whole island was poor. It is not endowed with the fertile plains of Corfu or Cephallonia, and the islanders have always had to wrench a living from the sea or the land. Even as late as 1970, road communications were very poor, and there are still problems with the water supply.

This lack of resources is apparent in the way the town was rebuilt after the

Aeria photograph of

earthquake; rather than demolishing the ruins and starting again, as was done in Zakynthos, the Lefkadans simply used what was left of the ground floor and built on a second storey with wood, mortar and sheets of metal.

This solution had two advantages: first, in the event of another earthquake the houses would be much safer, and second, it reduced building costs to a minimum.

The only really interesting buildings in Lefkada town are its churches, some of which we shall be describing. Most date from the late 17th or early 18th centuries.

As we approach the town of Lefkada from the direction of Vonitsa and reach the causeway, we see on our right the ruinous chapel of St Nicholas on the islet of the same name, close to the shore in shallow water.

The spot is associated with Angelos Sikelianos: the poet and his wife Eva spent some summers in the cottage which stands next to the chapel.

A little further along, a steep path up to the left leads to the chapel of St John, built in a cave which must once have been used by a hermit. There is a superb view from here.

On the landward side, the road along which we are driving was protected by the **New Fort** or **Griva Fort**. This is approached along a road which turns to the left just before the causeway begins, but for the time being entry is not permitted. Another name for the building is Fort Tekes: 'tekes' in Turkish means a monastery, and this was indeed an Orthodox foundation until 1807, when Ali Pasha of Ioannina converted it into a fort as part of his campaign of besieging the fort of Santa Maura.

Between here and the town of Lefkada we can see numerous traces of the attempts made since the Middle Ages to link the island to the mainland while at the same time keeping open the channel and allowing a close watch to be kept over ships sailing between Lefkada and the Akarnanian shore.

There are fortifications all the way along the channel, including —apart from Santa Maura itself— **Forts George** and **Alexander**, built during the brief Russian occupation of Lefkada.

The most interesting feature of the route over the causeway to Lefkada town is the **Fort of Santa Maura.**

The Fort stands 1,200 metres to the north east of Lefkada. It was built in the early 14th century by Giovanni Orsini in an attempt to deal with the pirate raids which were the scourge of the island. Standing as it does on an islet in the lagoon, it is an imposing ruin and an interesting example of the art of fortification in its time.

The period after 1300 was that in which the site of the capital of the island near the village of **Kalligoni**, where it had been since ancient times, was finally abandoned. The new city grew up around the walls of the castle, and was separated into two parts: Chora, which stood to the west where the channel is today, and **Alli Meria** to the east, in the direction of Akarnania.

In the south eastern corner of the castle is the **Chapel of Santa Maura**, which for many centuries gave its name not only to the castle but to the entire island. The church itself, built inside the castle wall, with a short entrance passage and a bell-tower, is of no particular interest, but it is connected with a fascinating story — or legend. Helen Palaiologus, the central though very shadowy figure in the story, was a member of one of the noblest families in Byzantium. In the late 15th century, she was sailing to Lefkada — to escape from the Turkish capture of Constantinople, according to one version, or to marry her daughter to the Count of Lefkada, in another.

The castle of Santa Maura; the entrance to the channel can also be seen.

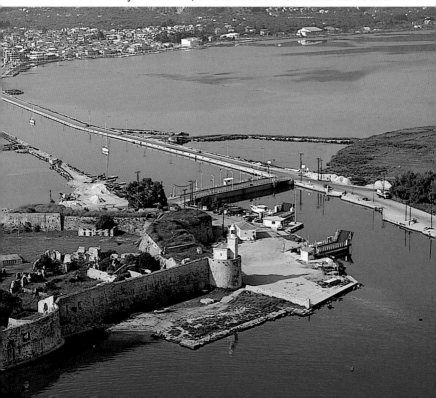

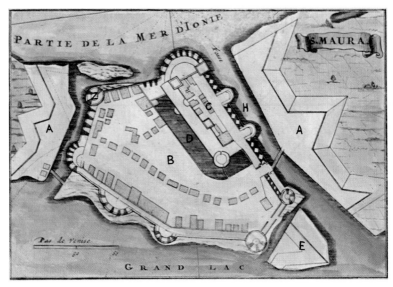

Santa Maura, in a drawing by Coronelli (1867).

However it may be, her ship was caught in a storm but managed to reach the island (all the versions agree on this point), either arriving on the feast-day of St Maura or carrying with it an icon of the Saint.

The name of St Maura is found elsewhere in the Ionian Islands, and there is a famous church to her at Mahairado on Zakynthos.

However, the traditional involvement of Helen Palaiologus cannot be entirely accurate, since we have at least four sources which call the castle 'Santa Maura' long before she ever sailed from Constantinople — one of these sources, in fact, dates from 120 years before that time. It may well be that when the iron-clad Anjou knights under Duke Walter II of Brienne took Lefkada in 1331 they named it Santa Maura after Sainte Maure, their home in France.

A century later, in 1479, the Turks took the castle and hundreds of Lefkadans were butchered. The church of St Maura became a mosque. In 1485, work began on an aqueduct with a length of more than three kilometres, and thousands of islanders were forced to help with the construction. The water was taken from the Megali Vrysi spring to the north west of the modern town, and eventually the aqueduct led to a kind of bridge with 360 arches which brought the water into the castle. It is said that Sultan Bayezid ordered his engineer to build this bridge wide enough to take a cart — the bridge was constructed exactly the width of a cart, which meant, of course, that it could not be used. The engineer paid for his mistake with his life. Traces of the Turkish aqueduct and bridge can still be seen in the **Yira** fish-farmand to the west of the modern road leading across the sea from the town to the castle.

In the period around 1700 the Venetians renovated and repaired the castle and in 1684 Morosini installed the lion of St Mark over the main gate.

Testimony to the strength of the fortifications can be seen in the fact that despite the repeated earthquakes which have struck the island, demolishing many of the buildings inside the castle, the walls themselves have suffered not a crack.

The castle had three lines of defence. The first one (marked A) consisted of strong stepped blocks, as can be seen on the plan, and the second (B) of the Old Fortress with seven bastions and cannon emplacements. Here there were water tanks, private houses and the two churches of St Maura (Orthodox) and Christ Pantocrator (Catholic). The Old Castle also had three schools: one Greek, one Catholic and one to train artillerymen.

The third and last line of defence was the inner fortress (the Castello, (C)' Here were the offices and residences of the authorities, barracks, a hospital, water tanks and powder magazines. Although the Venetians had modernised the castle in 1713, when they were forced to leave it they blew up some of the new features to prevent them falling into the hands of the Turks. However, the period of Turkish occupation —which cost the lives of 500 islanders and caused widespread destruction— lasted only a year, and the Venetians were soon back.

The eastern moat of the castle.

The castle of Santa Maura controls the passage from the mainland to the island, and so whoever holds it is also master of Lefkada. As a result, it has always been the first point of attack by invading forces, and much of the island's history has been written beneath its walls. On 16 March 1801, the flag of the Septinsular Republic was raised over it, ending centuries of slavery, but real liberation was to be a few more decades in coming.

Under the British protectorate of the 19th century, the moat (D) was filled in, and the area around the base of the south bastion became a cemetery. This, and another cemetery, are the only witnesses to the period of British occupation.

After the union of Lefkada with Greece in 1864, the castle was dis-

The Pantokrator bastion.

armed and its cannon removed. Some of them can still be seen within its perimeter, marked with the Venetian lion or the British crown, reminders of other ages — but not so far down in the world as to be used as bollards for ships to moor to.

A tremendous disaster occurred on 30 March 1888: the powder magazine caught fire, and the explosion demolished all the buildings inside the castle, together with the church of St Maura. The explosions and the fire even put the town itself in danger.

The church of St Maura was moved from the ruins to its present position, and in 1891 a lighthouse was built on the Pantocrator bastion (Z). In the years which followed, the castle continued to be used as a military camp, while in 1922 Greek refugees from

The causeway which links Lefkada to the mainland.

Asia Minor were settled there and lived in the castle for ten whole years.

Although it is protected by law as a monument, in 1938 more of the buildings were deliberately knocked down and the stone was sold off as building material.

During the Second World War, Santa Maura castle was bombed twice. The Italian forces of occupation have left their mark on it: the walls in some of the better-preserved chambers on the eastern side are covered with paintings and slogans.

To the east of the castle (H), on the landward side, is all that remains of the narrow passage through which ships passed before the opening of the Lefkada Channel, in 1905.

During the Festival of Speech and Music, in August, the castle of Santa Maura is used for many of the performances and it fills with life again — a reminiscence of its past days of glory and splendour.

As we leave the castle, we see on our right the outer harbour constructed by the British government of the Ionian Islands. It has a pier leading out to a lighthouse.

Until recently, the channel was crossed on one of the two chain-ferries, which can still be seen to the right of the floating bridge which replaced them. The chain-ferries are still used for exceptionally heavy vehicles.

We cross the bridge and turn left, heading along the causeway for the town.

The road leads over a little humpbacked bridge and ends at the harbour.

On the left as we approach Lefkada is the channel, and on the right is the lagoon, one of the most peaceful landscapes on the whole island. The lagoon has a depth of 0.30 - 0.60 metres throughout, and is used for fish farming.

Around it runs a strip of white sand, with a total length of 7 km. This is the Yira, whose sandy beaches are a favourite bathing-spot for the local people during the summer.

The road which runs round the Yira also leads eventually to Lefkada town. About halfway round is the little chapel of Our Lady, built in 1503, in a grove of weatherbeaten olive trees.

The chapel contains the family tomb of the Sikelianos family, but the great poet himself is not buried here.

As we continue around the Yira in a westerly direction, we come to a group of windmills.

There were originally twelve of them, all of which —for some reason— had Russian names: Orloff, Metzikoff, Kapetas, Moschovich, and so on. In March 1810, the British fought here the battle which was to prove decisive for their occupation of the island: with the help of the Greeks under Kolokotronis (who later became commander-in-chief of all the forces fighting to liberate Greece in

The western fish-farm of Lefkada.

the War of Independence of 1821), the British overcame Napoleon's French troops.

Immediately after the windmills is a turning to the right for the beach of Ayios Ioannis (2.5 km).

Here, at the foot of the rock on the eastern side of the bay, is the church of St Johhn 'Antzousis', which, according to tradition, was the first on the island. St Paul is said to have worshipped on the spot when on his way to Rome. The chapel which stands here today is supposed to have been built by the knights of Anjou, thus giving rise to the name.

One of the windmills on the Yira.

The church of St John 'Antzousis' huddled against its rock.

Yira and its excellent beach.
On the right, near the lagoon, the Church of
Our Lady with its little olive grove.

Plan
of the town

TOWN PLAN

1. The Bridge - The Way into
   the Town
2. Sikelianou Square
3. Bus Station - Busse
4. Agios Spyridonas
5. Museum of Folk-Art
6. Agios Nikolaos
7. Agios Dimitrios
8. Municipal Art Gallery
9. Haramogleios Library
10. Church of the Almighty
11. Presentation of the Virgin
12. Post Office
13. Agios Minas
14. Police
15. The Cathedral
16. Telecommunications
17. Town Hall
18. Archaeological Museum
19. Our Lady of the Strangers
20. Library
21. Ionian Bank
22. National Bank
23. Agricultural Bank
24. Prefectory
25. Hospital

As we enter the town by the direct route from the bridge, we come to a shady square —open on two sides— which contains the statues of three literary figures: Aristotelis Valaorities, Angelos Sikelianos and Lefkadio Hearn (see p. 47-49).

This part of the town, near its entrance, is of considerable interest to visitors because it contains most of the hotels (of a variety of categories), travel agencies, car rental offices and, of course, the harbour facilities. The caiques which tak e visitors on day-trips to Skorpios, Meganisi and elsewhere start from the very end of the quay.

Lefkada town is in a roughly rhomboid shape, one·vertex being the point where we enter from the causeway.

An aerial photograph of the town: below, the brid

The two sides of the vertex which converge here are the quayside road south, to the left, which goes to Ayia Kara, the fishermen's cafes and the modern marina, and the lagoon road, which leads west, to the prison, the Pouliou quarter and the Yira. They converge once more at the south-western extremity of the town, while the entire geographical shape is bisected by Dörpfeld Street —also known as the 'pazari— the main street of the town and the focus of life there.

The **bus-station** lies approximately half-way along the road to the left from the end of the bridge, which curves round the sea-front and is lined with fishing-boats and pleasure-craft.

ss which we enter the town, and the lagoon on the right.

We enter *Dörpfeld St* to the right of the large sea-front hotel. At first it is little more than a glorified alley, with souvenir shops and restaurants on both sides (note the fine fountain on the right-hand side). It soon leads us out into the town's main square, St Spyridon Square.

This is a pleasant open space with cafes where the local drink 'soumada' (made from almonds) can be tried. It is ideal as a place to sit and relax on a warm summer evening; all through the good weather, traffic is banned from the main street every evening so as to allow the 'volta' to take place. This evening promenade is a custom found throughout the Mediterranean and particularly popular in the Ionian Islands. It gives everyone a chance to meet friends and chat in a relaxed atmosphere, and in early —stricter— times it was the only type of social contact that boys and girls could have. So from early in the spring until late in the autumn, the chattering, carefree crowd strolls from one end of the street to the other, pausing now and then for refreshment in the square.

The church of St Spyridon stands on the north western side of the square. Visitors will notice at once that the churches of Lefkada differ from those of the mainland: instead of the usual Byzantine style with its domes, here the buildings are long and low, with their doors at the side.

This is not the only difference. The churches of Lefkada, like those of all

The Lower Fountain marks the start of the main street with the central squa

the Ionian area, date from Venetian times and the local architecture was strongly influenced by Italian models; as a result, the sculpture on the facades of the churches reminds us more of the Catholic West than the Orthodox East.

This impression is continued when we step inside the churches. Many are decorated with icons in which the impact of the West is very clear. The artists who decorated these churches belonged to what is called the 'Ionian School' of painting, in which the themes provided by the Orthodox Church were depicted in forms influenced by the Renaissance — the Renaissance which traditional Greek icon-painting rejected.

However, these Western influences do not make the churches any less 'Greek': the complicated carved screens, the candelabra, the portable icons and the black-clad priests always remind us that we are in an Orthodox place of worship. The main problem about visiting the churches of Lefkada is that since most are in private hands they are generally closed.

St Spyridon is one of these privately-owned churches. Built in the 17th century, it is one of the island's most interesting religious buildings, being particularly notable for its screen, by the wood-carver Groppas of Zakynthos, with icons by the local painter Gen. It also contains icons in the Western style of painting by the Lefkadan icon-painter Spyridon Gazis (1835-1920).

ening up in the background.

To the north west of the church of St Spyridon is the **Folklore Museum** operated by the Orpheus Association (open morning and evening in the summer; entrance free).

The Orpheus Music and Literary Association of Lefkada was founded in 1937, and its purpose was to encourage the intellectual and artistic development of the island. It runs a mixed choir, a mandolin choir, a school of music, a cinema club, the Folklore Museum, a radio station (Radio Orpheus) and theatrical and dance teams.

The Orpheus dance team was formed in 1960 with the purpose of preserving and disseminating the folk dances of Lefkada, the Ionian Islands and Greece as a whole.

The bedroom and the loom in the Folk Museum.

wide range of dances and have at their disposal a wardrobe of 180 traditional costumes from all over Greece. The dance team has a total strength of 120 performers of all ages.

The Orpheus Association has a number of highly-trained teachers who are engaged in a process of constant research into the world of Greek folk dance. This, with the enthusiasm of the dancers themselves, means that the Association's performances are technically superb and always well within the permitted bounds of tradition. Today the Orpheus Association team is widely regarded as one of the best that Greece can boast.

The Orpheus Association is a member of UNESCO's IOFA (International Organisation of Folk Arts). Since its foundation, it has taken part in all the festivals held in Greece and in many abroad, winning first prizes, distinctions and the acclaim of critics and the public alike.

Together with the entrance hall, the museum has a total of four rooms. The entrance hall contains a collection of old maps (dating from between 1687 and 1850) and photographs showing the island and the castle. Among them is the original of a superb map by the Venetian cosmographer Coronelli, dated 1687 (see p. 18). It will be seen from the map that the roads and paths on the island followed roughly the same courses as they do today, despite the fact that numerous placenames have changed. There is also a display cabinet with dolls dressed in traditional costume and arranged in a wedding procession.

To the right is a large room with a collection of domestic utensils and the tools used by Lefkadan farmers in times past, a superb loom which may be as much as two hundred years old,

The fireplace in the Folk Museum.

and models of an olive press and a windmill.

The first room to the left off the entrance hall has display cases full of outstanding local embroidery, the age of some of which is measured in centuries. The embroidery is worked with the greatest delicacy, and each piece must have required hundreds of hours of dedicated application. Also on display are some decorated knives from the village of Poros, which once specialised in this craft.

The last room has been set out as a typical Lefkadan village bedroom. Here, too, there are abundant embroideries, principally covers and cloths, but perhaps the most striking feature about the room is its light and airy atmosphere.

No one who would like to get some idea about how life used to be in Lefkada —and particularly those who are interested in the art of its women— can afford to miss the Museum.

We return to the main street, which is called S. Mela St after the square. Soon, on our left, we come to the **church of St Nicholas**, and a little further back from the main street, in among the alleys, is **St Demetrius**. To the right (north) is the **Municipal Library**, with a fine collection of post-Byzantine icons on the ground floor, while the church of **Our Lady of the Strangers** is a little further along.

St Demetrius was founded in 1688 and was a dependency of the 'Red Church' Monastery (see p.109). The church is small, but richly decorated. The screen was carved in 1870 by Panayiotis Prosalentis and contains much delicate work. The bishop's throne, in the Gothic style, is by the same wood-carver, while the icons which adorn the church were painted on plastered planks using the egg-and-tempera technique. The three icons showing scenes from the life of Christ, the work of Panayiotis Doxaras, are the island's oldest and date from the early 18th century.

To the south west of St Spyridon is the large square known as 'tou Marka', where the fish market used to be. In the third alleyway after the church is the **Municipal Art Gallery** and **Haramogleios Municipal Lefkadan Library**, created and donated to the town by Aristotelis A. Haramoglis. Its 28,000 items begin with the works of the local 5th century poetess Philaene, of particularly unrestrained language, and end with modern texts, all of the associated exclusively with Lefkada.

Mr Haramoglis began his collection in 1973. Less than a year later, when it contained 350 books, he decided that the endeavour upon which he had embarked should not be confined to his own personal pleasure.

He then began a tireless hunt to bring together whatever material about Lefkada or originating on the island he was able to find in bookshops, libraries and even junk shops all over Greece and abroad. His efforts lasted 18 years and the collection now contains approximately 22,000 titles dating back as far as 1420.

The collection has now been donated to the Municipality of Lefkada (for which Mr Haramoglis received an award from the Athens Academy) and contains:

1. Books by 750 Lefkadan authors.
2. Books by non-Lefkadans on Lefkada and the Lefkandans, divided among 82 different units.
3. Engravings and maps dating from between 1420 and 1900.
4. Postcards from 1895 to the present day.
5. The titles of Lefkadan newspapers dating from 1866 to the present day, with 2,500 specimen copies.
6. Titles of Greek and foreign periodicals, with 3,500 copies.
7. Specimens of Lefkadan newspapers.
8. Various items of printed matter and other objects from recent times.
9. Farming and agricultural books not related to Lefkada but intended to assist the island's development.

An engraving from O. Dapper's "Naukeurice Beschryving von Morea peloponnesus: en de Ellanden, Gelegen onder de Kusten von Morea... Corfu, Cefalonia, S. Maura, Zanten", Amsterdam 1688

A map engraved by Mattaus Morian, Frankfurt 1645 - Newe Arcmontolgia Cosmica.

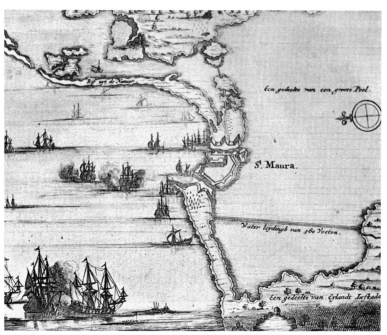

The church of the Pantokrator, behind whose altar Valaoritis is buried.

As we walk along the main street after the square, we will note the incredible variety of shops beneath the pleasant arcades. It is literally possible to buy everything from a computer to a bell to put round the neck of a goat. Further along, on the left, is the **church of Christ Pantocrator.**

This is the private church of the Valaoritis family. It was founded in the early 18th century and took its final form in 1830, although the interesting decorated facade is later work, dating from 1890. In the church are the tombs of well-known Lefkadans (A. Halkiopoulos, A. Stavros, D. and P. Petritsopoulos) while behind the altar is the tomb of the great poet Aristotelis Valaoritis himself.

The church has a fine screen dating from about 1860: it is in the neo-Classical style, and prefigured the work to be done later in that manner by the Prosalentis family and Vretos. The paintings are the work of Spyridon Ventouras and Dionysios Kalivokas of Zakynthos (the latter of whom painted the ceiling). The bishop's throne also has interesting decoration.

A little further along the main street, on the left, is the **church of the Presentation of the Virgin**. The church we see today dates from the late 18th century, and replaced an earlier structure of 1720. It has the only stone-built bell-tower in the town.

The interior of the church was painted in about 1815, and the best icon-painters of Lefkada worked on it. There is a most impressive Second Coming, which covers almost all the pediment of the screen. The screen itself, in a baroque style, is one of the island's finest, and the ceiling has copies by Spyridon Gazis of paintings by Raphael.

St Minas, at one end of the main street; the other is at the harbour.

The Post Office, the banks and the exhibition of local handicrafts will also be found along the main street.

The main street ends at the church of St Minas, in the square by the same name. Here, every morning, there is a market to which farmers from the suburbs of the town and the outlying villages bring their products.

The **church of St Minas** was built in 1707. Its carved wooden screen and its paintings make it the most interesting ecclesiastical monument in the town. The screen, the work of craftsmen from Zakynthos, is a fine example of the baroque style of the third decade of the 18th century. The paintings, also 18th century, are by Konstantinos Kontarinis, one of the most representative painters of the post-Byzantine style; his attempt to preserve the Orthodox concept of art while at the same time incorporating Italian influence is clear. The church also contains paintings by I. Rousos, N. Doxaras and N. Koutouzis, the latter two of whom painted the ceiling. The balcony of the women's gallery has paintings by Ventouras. The bishop's throne and the two icon-stands are by I. Vretos (1935), while the Easter catafalque and the candelabra are by Efstratios Prosalentis (1818).

Near the church of Christ Pantocrator, about half-way along the main street, we can turn down narrow Mitropoleos St. This is the location of the **police station** and, a little further along, the modern **Cathedral**.

Turning right (rather than left in the direction of the cathedral) brings us to the telephone company **(OTE)** building and the Town Hall, which is housed in a 19th century British building.

The road past the **Town Hall** leads west to the **Archaeological Museum**, which has a small but interesting collection of finds discovered by Dörpfeld in approximately 30 royal tombs of the 12th century BC which came to light at Nidri, items found in a cave close to Evyiros (in the south of the island) and other finds from a cave at Frini, close to the town.

The investigation of this cave, which has a narrow entrance and numerous galleries, has never been completed. In antiquity it seems to have been a place of worship. The gold leaves on the right-hand side of the single room in which the archaeological collection is exhibited are from recent excavations at Karyotes. They date from the Classical or Hellenistic periods, and were found in a large cemetery discovered in this part of the island, which has produced many other finds in the Museum. Note also the photographs taken when Dörpfeld was digging at Nidri — when the village consisted of no more than a handful of huts!

The relative poverty of the archaeological collection is partially explained by the fact that many objects found on Lefkada have been moved to the archaeological museums of Athens and Ioannina.

Marinou St takes us from the square in which the telephone company and the Town Hall are located to **Our Lady of the Strangers** or the **Nativity of the Virgin**, an 18th century church which took its final form in 1836.

Its screen is reputed to be the first work by Efstratios Prosalentis, and the church also contains interesting icons painted by various Lefkadan artists. The ceiling and parts of the walls were

From the Museum of Post-Byzantine Art: a work by Andreas Moraitis (18th century).

painted by Spyridon Gazis.

Very close to Our Lady of the Strangers is a fine 19th century building containing the **Municipal Library** and the **Gallery of Post-Byzantine Art**.

The Municipal Library was founded in the early 1950s with the remainder of the collection which had been in the library of the Lefkada Club, looted by the Italian occupation authorities in 1941. It contains old books and manuscripts.

At about this time, the efforts of Bishop Dorotheos and Professor P. G. Rontoyannis led to the founding of the Gallery of Post-Byzantine Art, which contains icons donated to various churches on the island by local families.

The areas to the north and south of the main street in Lefkada town are crammed with little houses, very few of them more than two storeys high, lining narrow alleys.

Each house has its own microscopic courtyard, full of flowers and pot plants. The upper storeys of these houses are usually simple structures made of brick and wood for protection against earthquakes. The underlying structure is then covered with metal sheeting, giving the entire area a light and airy feeling.

Note the way in which the window frames, the shutters and often the beams are picked out in different colours, usually shades of green or brown. Here and there, a heavier, thicker wall testifies to the fact that a

Our Lady 'Hodeghetria' from the east.

more imposing residence once stood on the site.

Before concluding this description of the town, there are two more sights which should be covered.

The first of these lies some 200-300 metres beyond St Minas, on the road to the cemetery. Here is the cafe of Pallas, where the local almond drink called 'soumada' can be sampled. Opposite, among the olive trees, the older men still play the game callled 'balles' or 't'ambali', which is purely local and is played with egg-shaped balls on a concave pitch. The game is found nowhere else in Greece and is of unknown origin.

Two kilometres further south, in an olive grove, stands all that is left of the Monastery of Our Lady 'Hodeghetria', dating back to 1450. It is amazing that after all these centuries and so many earthquakes, which laid waste large parts of the island, the main church of the monastery is still standing.

This church, a single-aisled structure with a wooden roof, is the oldest Christian monument on Lefkada. A considerable part of the wall-paintings on the north, east and west walls inside has survived and is of the greatest beauty and significance.

The church is connected with a variation on the Helen Palaiologus myth with which the castle is also associated. According to this legend, Helen retired here as a nun in 1486, after the death of the daughter she had married to Duke Leonard III Tocco of Lefkada (see p. 16).

ROUTES ON THE ISLAND

Only a few years ago, most of the roads on Lefkada were in very poor condition; journeys of any length were an exhausting business, and it was difficult to visit and enjoy the beauties of the island. Today, the road network has been significantly improved; the main roads are all properly surfaced, and even the dirt roads are generally passable. Now it is easy to drive right around the island even in the course of a day; all its beauties and magic can be sampled with ease, its verdant woods, superb beaches and attractive villages can be visited, and visitors can make friends with the hospitable islanders.

All our routes start in the town of Lefkada; we begin on the north western coast, continue with the eastern part of the island and then —still moving in a circular fashion— the centre.

The routes are arranged as follows:

1. Faneromeni Monastery - Ayios Nikitas - Kathisma - Kalamitsi.. 86

2. Lazarata - Hortata - Athani - Egremni - Porto Katsiki - Cape Lefkatas 97

3. Lefkada - Karya - Platystoma - Engluvi - Vafkeri - Alexandros 106

4. Lefkada - Nydri - Ayia Kiriaki - Madouri - Skorpios - Meganisi 112

5. Nydri - Poros - Syvota - Basiliki - Syvros - Ayios Petros 130

A number of short trip from Nydri (Route 4) and Vasililiki (Route 5) into the surrounding areas, which are of great interest.

ROUTE 1

Lefkada - Faneromeni Monastery - Ayios Nikitas - Kathisma - Kalamitsi

This route takes us to a historic monastery and then to two of the finest beaches on the island. For those who do not have transport of their own, the monastery is only a short taxi ride from the town. There are also buses which pass the monastery on the way to Ayios Nikitas.

We leave the town along Angelou Sikelianou Ave., fork left at the court-house and then turn right (signpost).

The icon of Our Lady 'Faneromeni'.

After passing the Archaeological Museum we pass through the western suburbs of the town.

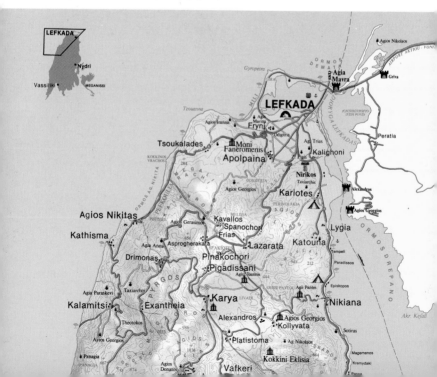

2 km: The area between here and the pretty suburb of **Frini** is ideal for walks. The trees cast dense shade and both Frini and the nearby village of Apolpaina are of considerable interest.

After Frini, the road begins to climb sharply. There is a very beautiful view over Lefkada and across to the mainland, and this, too, is a nice place for walks among the pine woods.

3 km: The **Monastery of Our Lady 'Faneromeni'**, close to the town, has a superb view.

The foundation was set up around the mid-17th century, and until 1760 it was in private ownershp. The building we see today was rebuilt in the late 19th century after two fires, and it bears marked traces of the influence of the architecture of Zakynthos. The icon of Our Lady also dates from this period, while the screen, by Efstratios Prosalentis, is of outstanding interest. The trees around the Monastery were planted by the Bishopric of Lefkada in the period between 1940 and 1960; as a result, the Monastery has much more for the visitor than its history.

The dense pinewood is ideal for walks, and there is a panoramic view. In 1968, the buildings were renovated once again, and, thanks to the interest shown by the monks, Faneromeni is one of the main destinations for pilgrims on Lefkada. Each year there is a major feast on the holiday of the Holy Trinity.

The 'Faneromeni' Monastery, with the Yira in the background.

The city and the channel from the 'Faneromeni' Monastery.

Aerial photograph of Tsoukalades.

6 km: The road continues to climb amongst olive groves, and soon reaches **Tsoukalades**, a peaceful little village devoted entirely to agriculture. Here the vegetation changes, with olives giving way to the pines which cloak the steep and rock slopes leading down to the north west coast.

After Tsoukalades we top a low hill and begin to descend. Soon a superb view of the long beach of **Pevkoulia** opens out before us, with the village of Ayios Nikitas in the background.

On the left, the main road passes a track which leads up through the beautiful pine forest to Asproyerakata (see p. 98).

The beach between here and Ayios Nikitas is at least 4 km in length; we come down to sea level about halfway along and continue on the coast as far as Ayios Nikitas.

The red stone in the area is striking.

The immense beach at Pefkoulia.

Ayios Nikitas under the shadow of the cliff with its windmill.

St Nikitas and its attractive beach, with the coastline stretching along to Pefkoulia in the background.

12 km: Ayios Nikitas has grown from a quiet fishing village into one of the island's main resort areas, and, to judge by the amount of building activity in progress, can be expected to develop still further in the future. The nucleus of the village, however, has been placed under a preservation order.

Apart from the long beach which we have already seen, there is also a pretty little beach right in front of the village, with the rocky cape of Ayios Nikitas on the left. The village has all the infrastructure necessary for visitors (hotels, rooms to rent, restaurants) and there is a community-run camp site in the olives on the upper side of the road as we enter.

Since Ayios Nikitas is very busy in summer, parking can be very difficult. Visitors should also bear in mind that the main road through the village is a dead end, and very narrow; if taken by mistake, there is nowhere to turn round.

Ayios Nikitas is an ideal place for those whose summer holidays focus around swimming and sunbathing; the landscape, too, is particularly impressive, and there is a fair degree of nightlife. Ayios Nikitas, however, is not the only superb beach in the area.

14 km: We continue past Ayios Nikitas; after 2 km, a road turns off to the right through the sand-hills and ends above the outstanding beach of **Kathisma**.

This vast expanse of golden sand and azure water is really a continuation of Ayios Nikitas beach after the interruption of the headland cliffs, now on our right.

A rough track leads down to the beach and ends there.

Kathisma: between the mountains and the sea.

On the right, as we have said, the beach ends at the rocks (which run quite a long way out to sea, with little caves and coves: a superb place for swimming), but to the left it stretches away almost endlessly. In effect, it is the same beach which can be reached from Kalamitsi, the next village to the south. Off the beach on this side are some little rocky islets where bats nest; at dusk, they can be seen heading in flocks for the vineyards which lie at the top of the beach. The sunset at Kathisma is unforgettable.

The western beaches of Lefkada are among the island's finest features, and it is strange that they have remained 'undeveloped' for so long; very few of them have even rudimentary facilities. On the other hand, the sea here is often much rougher than at the more sheltered beaches on the east coast. Today,

the roads to even the most isolated beaches —down towards Cape Lefkatas— are relatively good, and the solitude which was one of their beauties will, presumably, soon be a thing of the past.

We return to the road from Ayios Nikitas and begin to climb through the pine trees on the way to Kalamitsi.

23 km: Kalamitsi. On the slopes of Mt Rachi, is hidden from the sea. The site was chosen to protect the inhabitants from pirates. In former times, this was a large and important place, and had a school as far back as 1825.

Wheat was grown in the vicinity, as can be seen from the large number of ruined windmills. the village has a number of churches amd chapels.

One of the chapels, that o Our Lady 'of the Gardens', used to be a monastery with seven cells. It was built by a local family which wanted to protect its lands: monasteries were given special privileges by the conquerors. In 1620, it collapsed and was rebuilt subsequently coming —with its lands— unter the control of the Faneromeni's monastery. Later when the monastery's lands were divided up among the villagers Our Lady declined and is now only a chapel.

This village stands on a saddle above the sea, over which it gives the impression of hovering. From the upper part of the village, near the water tank, there is a marvellous view down to the beaches.

Kalamitsi is almost untouched by tourism: an ideal place to wander through the alleyways and see what everyday life in a simple Lefkadan village is like. Kalamitsi is also well-known for the quality of its woven goods.

There is a crossroads in the middle of the village.

Going straight ahead soon leads us out of the village and back down in the direction of the sea. The road, which is not surfaced all the way, brings us after 4 km to a series of sandy coves. Apart from the high season, this is another ideal place for those who prefer their own company when swimming.

We return to the crossroads. The road to the left (as we come from Ayios Nikitas) joins the main west coast road, and we can return to Lefkada town via Asproyerakata and Lazarata (see route 2, p. 98).

Below Kalamitsi: the beach with the crystal-clear waters of the Ionian.

ROUTE 2

Lefkada -Lazarata - Hortata - Athani - Egremni - Porto Katsiki - Cape Lefkatas

This route takes us the length of the western coast of Lefkada. Here, the clean open sea sets off the steep cliffs and combines with them to create a landscape of startling intensity. The long beaches are covered with delicate, crystalline sand.

Our route runs through some fine scenery and attractive villages before ending at Cape Lefkatas, the southern-most extremity of the island, in an area of great natural beauty and historical interest.

We leave the town by the Nidri road (left at the end of the causeway, along the seafront and left again at the crossroads). Just outside the town, we turn right, on the road signposted Karya. The road begins to climb almost immediately, winding up through olive groves amid most attractive scenery. These fertile slopes give us a fine view down over the town of Lefkada and the vast olive grove which lies behind it.

Porto Katsiki: one of the superb beaches along the steep west coast.

9 km: Turning, right, for the nearby village of **Spanochori**, which can be seen on the hilltop. This is the first of a series of villages (the others are Lazarata, Fryas, Kavallos and Asproyerakata) which stand in a fertile and highly cultivated plain.

The area is known generally as 'Sfakiotes', and according to tradition takes its name from a group of settlers who moved here from Sfakia in Crete in the 16th or 17th century. As one might expect, these are agricultural communities which the out side world has barely touched. Spanochori has a particularly fine view down over Lefkada down.

10 km: We continue along the main road and reach **Lazarata**. The road through the Sfakiotes district bears right here, and after a further 2 km comes to Asproyerakata. Here the bright green of the fields —or rather, gardens: crops of different kinds grow side by side— contrasts with the silvery green of the olive groves which we left behind on the way up from the coast and the bare hillside which we shall soon be traversing.

12 km: Asproyerakata has a pleasant shady square where we can rest and where food is available. After a further two kilometres, we fork right, leaving the road to Karya (see route 3).

The road heads west after Asproyerakata and then turns south. It runs parallel to the coast and at some distance from the cliffs which plunge down into the sea. At one point, however, there is a superb view over Ayios Nikitas and its beach. The landscape here is rather desolate and the signs of depopulation are everywhere to be seen, in the overgrown terraces and abandoned fields.

Lazarata, built by people from Sfakia in Crete, or from Epirus.

Hortata was the creation of refugees from southern Italy and Avlon.

19 km: The only villages along this stretch of road are **Drymonas** and a little further along, **Exantheia** (21 km), a village with a Byzantine name and a very long history. Both these villages are built in positions which afford the maximum protection from the weather, nestling into the hillside. A road to the right leads to Kalamitsi (route 1, p. 94).

29 km: After the turning for Kalamitsi, the road continues through the fields to the large village of **Hortata**.

This community stands on a very pleasant site with a magnificent view south and west, over a landscape which gradually declines in the direction of Cape Lefkatas. Food is available in the pretty cafes of the village. Walkers could follow the track up to the east of the village, which leads across the mountains to the plateau above Englouvi.

Immediately after Hortata is the turning for **Ayios Vasileios, Manasi** and **Nikoli,** half-forgotten and almost empty settlements along a track which leads to the large village of Ayios Petros, in the direction of Vasiliki.

30 km: Before long, we come to a crossroads. The road to Cape Lefkatas bears right, passing through the hamlet of **Kamilio** before running along the low range of hills which forms the spine of Lefkada's southernmost part.

There are only two villages in this area: **Dragano,** 4 km after the crossroads, and **Athani,** 2 km further on. The buses only go as far as Athani, which is developing into something of a centre for visitors heading for the superb beaches of Yialos, Egremni and Porto Katsiki.

For the time being, though, Athani has rather a limited range of facilities.

From Athani there is access to Yialos, part of the enormous beach which runs all the way along the west coast of the island. After we pass the last house in the village, a track leads off to the right down to the edge of the rocks. This beach is completely deserted and as beautiful as any other part of the coastline.

The magnificent beaches of Egremni and Porto Katsiki are beyond Athani, at a distance which makes some form of transport essential.

38 km: The first beach we come to is **Egremni**, beyond Athani on the right (signpost). The track starts off smoothly enough, but it soon begins to plunge steeply downwards and, after about 2.5 km, ends in a sharply sloping open space from which a variety of so-called paths lead precipitously down to the beach. From above, the beach is hard to resist; there is a long strip of golden sand, the water is a deep blue colour, and, like all the western beaches, there is usually a fringe of waves. Egremni is undoubtedly a place for those who prize their solitude above everything else.

40 km: Further to the south of Egremni is **Porto Katsiki**, perhaps the island's finest beach and a good deal more accessible. The track down to Porto Katsiki leaves the Cape Lefkatas road about 2 km beyond Egremni (signpost).

The beach at Engremni.

It descends gently, crossing a bare hillside before ending in a large car park. To the left, there are steps down to the superb beach, with high white cliffs in the background. On the right, more steps and a cement walkway lead out to a little headland (with an excellent view across to the beach). Despite the relative length of the journey (40 km from Lefkada town) and the need for some form of transport (though, as noted elsewhere, there are boat trips from Vasiliki and even Nidri) Porto Katsiki is a place which no visitor to Lefkada should miss.

The main road (or rather, track) carries on after the Porto Katsiki turning in the direction of Cape Lefkatas. Since Komilio we have been following the western side of the range of hills down the peninsula, and it is only as we approach its southernmost tip that we see Vasiliki Bay for the first time. The road descends a hillside and reaches a fork. Turning left brings us to a last isolated farm and the **Monastery of St Nicholas,** a dilapidated group of buildings.

Trips to Porto Katsiki can be arranged from all over the island.

50 km: The right-hand road at the fork before the monastery soon brings us to the southernmost tip of the island, opposite Cephallonia, **Cape Lefkatas, Nira, Kavo tis Kyras** or **Kavo Dukato.** This is the most prominent headland on all Lefkada and it was among the most famous cliffs in antiquity, probably being what Homer referred to as 'the white stones'. It consists of white cliffs towering 60 metres above the foaming waves of the Ionian sea: a terrible passage for seafarers.

In very early times, around 1200 BC, sacrifices were made here to appease the gods and the Spirit of the Storm. By the Classical period, around 400 BC, the human victims of the early period had been replaced by convicted criminals who were also given some chance of saving themselves: before the victim was thrown from the cliff, feathers and live birds were tied around his body, thus ensuring that he hit the sea a little more gently. Beneath, boats awaited to provide first aid if he survived — in which case his life was spared.

Apollo, apart from his other capacities, was also a maritime god, the patron of sea-farers, and he was worshipped as 'Apollo of the Dolphins'. It was in this guise that he replaced earlier cults at the sanctuary on Cape Lefkatas, which was famous throughout the ancient world. Each year there was a feast in honour of the god, attended by pilgrims from all over Greece. It may have been held in early spring.

Apollo was, however, primarily the god of purification and healing — of the mind as well as the body. It is to him that the leap from a cliff, as a means of releasing oneself from the torments of love, is attributed.

According to the ancient myths, the goddess Aphrodite was the first to jump from Cape Lefkatas, to cure herself from her love of Adonis, whom death had snatched from her. By the 6th century AD the lover's leap had become a widespread tradition, to judge from the frequency with which the ancient poets mention it. It is this tradition which Sappho refers to in her poems, giving rise to the legend that she herself jumped into the sea from Cape Lefkatas.

Sappho was the greatest poetess of antiquity, often being referred to as 'the tenth Muse'. She made the cape universally famous, and attached her name to it: **'Kavos tis Kyras'** means 'the Lady's Cape'. The story about her love for Phaon has its roots in some erotic lines by her, and the myth that she threw herself from the rocks at Cape Lefkatas came down to us, still vivid, through Latin literature. The story of 'the Lady' lived on as a folk tale down to the recent past: here is is, as recorded in one of the villages in the Athani-Dragano area:

Once upon the time there was a queen, and she made a law saying that anyone who erred should be flung from the cliff at Cape Lefkatas. But, as luck would have it, she was the first person to fall into error — by being unfaithful to her husband. Everyone pleaded with her not to jump, but she insisted that the law must be obeyed. So they tied feathers and live birds to her body and spread sails out below her so that she might fall softly. But the queen was killed, and ever since the cliff has been called 'the Lady's Cape'.

Today there is no trace of the temple of Apollo, and a modern lighthouse stands on the site. We encounter the Sappho myth once more, with a reference to the beauty of the spot, in Byron's Childe Harold (1812); Byron

Sappho plunging from the cliff at Cape Lefkatas (engraving, 1913).

sailed this way the first time he came to Greece.

XXIX
Childe Harold sail'd,
and pass'd the barren spot
Where sad Penelope o'erlook'd
the wave;
And onward view'd the mount, not yet
forgot,

The lover's refuge, and the Lesbian's
grave.
Dark Sappho! cound not verse immor-
tal save
That breast imbued with such immor-
tal fire?
Could she not live who life
eternal gave?
If life eternal may await the lyre,

Cape Lefkatas

That only Heaven to which Earth's children may aspire.

XL
'Twas on a Grecian autumn's
gentle eve
Childe Harold hail'd Leucadia's cape
afar'
A spot he long'd to see, nor cared to
leave:
Oft did he mark the scenes of vanish'd
war,
Actium, Lepanto, fatal Trafalgar;
Mark them unmoved, for he would not
delight
(Born beneath some remote inglorious
star)
In themes of bloody fray, or gallant
fight,
But loathed the bravo's trade, and
laughed at martial wight.

XLI
But when he saw the evening star above
Leucadia's far-projecting rock of woe,
And hail'd the last resort of fruitless
love,
He felt, or deem'd he felt, no common
glow
And as the stately vessel glided slow
Beneath the shadow of that ancient
mount,
He watch'd the billow' melancholy
flow,
And, sunk albeit in thought as he was
wont,
More placid seem'd his eye, and smooth
his pallid front.

(Canto II)

Today, "stately vessels" still pass out at sea: the car ferries to Italy. *Cape Lefkatas has an excellent view south, in the direction of Cephallonia and Ithaca, and the sunsets are famous.*

This is where our route ends; we must now return by the route along which we came, to the top of the peninsula.

105

ROUTE 3
(the centre of the island)

Lefkada - Karya - Englouvi - Platystoma - Vafkeri - Alexandros

Although the farming communities around the Karya plateau have fallen prey to depopulation, a visit to the area is of the greatest interest. The natural environment is of great beauty, the routes we shall be taking are impressive and the villages are attractively traditional. In addition, it would be a serious omission to come to Lefkada and not visit **Karya** to see the wonderful traditional lacework.

Although accommodation is available in these villages (in the form of 'hostels'), the distances from the coast up to the centre of the island are not so great as to make day-trips impossible.

We leave Lefkada town along the Nidri road and soon bear right for Karya, as in Route 2. At Asproyerakata we take the left fork (signposted for Karya). Almost immediately after this is a turning to the left with the signpost Pinakochori.

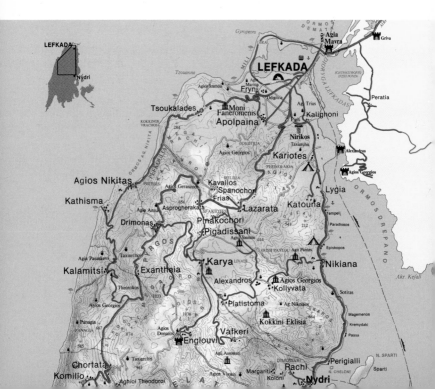

The windmills at Sfakiotis, reminder of an earlier age.

11 km: Pinakochori itself is not of any particular interest, but the road through the village (which leads to Lazarata) provides us with a superb view over the plateau in the heart of the island. From here we can see immediately how these villages came to be located here.

Down and to our left, among the low hills, is a kind of basin with a diameter of approximately five kilometres which is intensively cultivated. Crops such as wheat need to be at a certain altitude, and until it became unprofitable to do so areas such as this produced cereals for the whole of Lefkada.

The windmills which can be seen here and there across the plateau are evidence of the extent of wheat-growing.

To the east, the plateau comes to an end in a series of low hills among which villages nestle, while to the west the villages are located on slopes too steep to cultivate. The shortage of land meant that not an inch of soil which could be used for crops could be wasted.

To the south of Pinakochori, at Livadi, is the ruined —but once rich— **monastery of St John the Divine**. It was founded in the 17th century, but the church we see today is a more modern building.

On the walls, whitewashed paintings can be distinguished. The church contains the tomb of the warrior Simos Bouas (d. 1622).

12 km: we return to the main road, pass through **Pigadisani**, a microscopic hamlet clinging to the hillside, and get our first real view of Karyua.

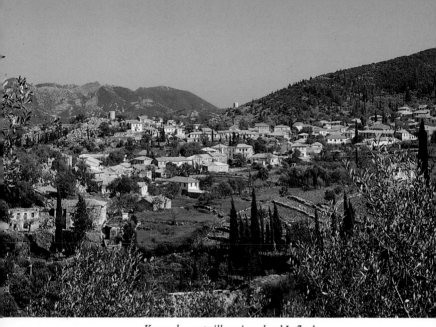

Karya, largest village in upland Lefkada.

14 km: Karya. This is the principal village in the upland part of the island and it has managed to retain some of its vitality. Traditions are kept up: on 11 August each year, there is a reconstruction of a typical Lefkadan wedding, and those who are on the island at the time will find it worth a visit.

Karya consists of a number of 'neighbourhoods' arranged around an attractive paved main square shaded by huge trees. However, the square is not at the centre of the village, which may give a mistaken impression of the size of the community.

In fact, Karya goes on for a long way after the square, and there are interesting walks along its sloping streets and alleys.

Karya is known principally for its lace and embroidery, which may be bought in the village itself (wherever the sign 'KENTHMATA' is displayed) or at the showroom in the main street of Lefkada town. There are also some superb examples in the Folklore Museum (see p. 77, in the description of Lefkada town).

A piece of lace from Karya undoubtedly makes an unusual souvenir, and by buying it one is contributing to keeping alive a tradition which would otherwise be dying out: the younger women of the village are not always content simply to carry on the handicraft tradition.

Just before we enter Karya there is a turning to the right.

This road leads up into the mountains to the top of Mt Ayios Ilias, and one could continue along and down to Englouvi. However, the road is also

The shady square at Karya.

Bell-tower at Alexandros.

used for access to the military installations on the summit, and —strictly speaking— civilian traffic is banned. However, travellers are usually allowed to pass.

We leave Karya along the continuation of its main street. The road now runs down into the plain, and there is a fork. To the left will take us to Platystomo and Vafkeri, while the main road continues to Englouvi.

17 km: Taking the left fork, we head south east in the direction of **Platystomo**, a nearly empty village whose few remaining inhabitants are all elderly.

Here there is a crossroads: to the right, the road goes to Vafkeri (see below), and straight ahead leads down the mountain to Periyali, near Nidri (see Route 4).

19 km: We take the road to the left in Platystomo, which crosses the plain to **Alexandros**, a sad place with only a handful of inhabitants. The rest of the villagers moved to the east and built the village of Nikiana (see p. 114) on the coast.

It really seems a pity that Alexandros shold have been abandoned, for the houses, gradually falling to pieces, show what a pretty place it must once have been. The village stands among shady olive groves.

To the south east of Alexandros, about half an hour away on foot, is the **Monastery of Our Lady**, also known as the **'Red Church'**. The foundation is in ruins, and only the church survives in a gully on the western side of Mt Skaros.

Shortly after Alexandros to the east

is a turning for yet another depopulated village, **Kollyvata**.

Close to Kollyvata and 1.5 km from Alexandros is one of the island's most historic monasteries, that of **St George Skarous**. This was founded before 1500, probably by shepherds. It stands on an outcrop on the west side of Mt Skaros, the main mountain mass of this part of the island. The monastery was a major local landowner, but its estates were broken up and distributed to landless farmers in 1928. The priest of Alexandros, who was also the last abbot of the monastery, died in 1964.

The church has interesting wall-painting dating from around 1620. Kollyvata is linked to the east coast of the island by a road which comes down at Nikiana.

After Alexandros, the 'main road' continues around the perimeter of the plateau, eventually bringing us back to Lazarata near the beginning of the route.

None of the roads described above is surfaced, but they are all in relatively good condition and should cause drivers no problems.

We return to the fork outside Karya and head south, along the road to the right, which runs through woods amid a most attractive landscape before turning to enter Englouvi.

19 km: Englouvi, the highest village on Lefkada at an altitude of 730 metres. Its situation, among low hills, is rather peculiar, and as one walks through the village one is constantly coming upon groups of houses in places where one would never have

expected they might be. Here, the houses are strongly built of stone: although the climate of the Ionian Islands is generally mild, up here the winter is no joke. It is an indication of the degree of depopulation that while before the War there were 200 schoolchildren in Englouvi, the school has now closed completely.

Englouvi is famous throughout Lefkada not for its arts and crafts, as with the lace of Karya, but for the excellent quality of its lentils — which the locals claim are the best produced in Greece (they have prizes to prove it, too).

The fields where the lentils and other crops are grown are in two areas: the first is to the south of the village, in the little valley which slopes up into the hills. The second (and more interesting) can be reached by taking the road which turns sharp right in the village opposite the cafe. This climbs up out of Englouvi and, after about 2 kilometers, reaches a high plateau covered with fields. Here is the chapel of St Donatus, where each year there is a feast at which the local lentils, cooked in an enormous pot, are consumed.

A little further on are the remains of a huge (probably pre-Roman) tower, from which according to tradition Bishop Donatus was flung and killed during a persecution of the Christians. In the summer, when the fields are empty and dry, the barren landscape is striking and unusual.

To the north of Englouvi itself, the scenery is dominated by the chapel of the Prophet Elijah, perched on a seemingly inaccessible peak. One can feel only admiration for the forefathers of the villagers, who managed to haul up to such a place all the materials needed

Englouvi: landscape and streets.

to build the chapel. Unfortunately the remainder of the summit ridge of Ayios Ilias, looming above the village, is occupied by a gigantic radar station which completely spoils the beauty of the landscape.

To return to the Karya plateau without retracing our steps, we can continue along the track which runs through the centre of the village. After some sharp bends, this bears to the left and begins to descend the hillside, with superb views out over the plain. Nidri can just be picked out far to the east.

This road goes gently down in the direction of Vafkeri. Shortly before we reach the village, a path (to the right at the water tank) leads through vineyards and fields (30 mins. on foot) to the deserted, ruined monastery of the Archangels. This was founded in the 16th century. The main church, with its wall-paintings, is still standing but in poor condition.

21 km: Vafkeri. The history of this village goes back to the 16th-17th centuries, but now most of its houses stand empty. It is yet another of the villages which are slowly dying of depopulation.

To the east of Vafkeri, the road continues down to Nidri and the east coast.

We can also return by heading north from Vafkeri, through Alexandros and Lazarata, before rejoining the main road to Lefkada town.

ROUTE 4

Lefkada - Nikiana - Nidri
Short trips from Nidri:
(the waterfall, St Kyriake,
Niochori) - **Nearby islands:**
(Madouri, Skorpios, Meganisi)

The east coast of Lefkada is the part
of the island which has been most
intensively developed for tourism,
and it is easy to see why. This part of
the island is the greenest — resem-
bling in that respect the other Ionian
islands, and Corfu in particular — and
it has many good beaches.

All the little villages which we shall
be encountering along the coast as we
head for Nidri correspond to villages
up on the mountain. The land at Periyali, for example, belongs to the villagers of Platystomo, while the Nidri
area was the property of Vafkeri. In
the past, the coastal areas were used as
farmland, and the owners of the fields
lived up in their mountain villages.
But since the area entered its stage of
'development' the villagers from up
on the mountain have moved down to
the coast and live there more or less
permanently — which, of course, has
meant that villages such as Vafkeri
and Platystomo have declined.

The wooded hills which rise behind
the coast mean that this trip runs
through impressive scenery. The
changing landscape —dominated
now by the hills and now by the sea—
leads in the end to the peaceful bay of
Vlicho and to **Yeni,** a little promon-
tory whose special natural beauty has
caused it to be classed as a protected
area.

Traces of antiquity outside Kalligoni.

2 km: We leave the town of Lefkada along the sea-front (past the bus station) and turn left at the crossroads, as usual. Leaving the road to Karya on our right (see Route 3), we run through olive groves close to the sea before reaching **Kaligoni,** a little settlement to the south of Lefkada town.

On a hill-top near here are the remains of **ancient Nericus,** the capital of the surrounding area after the 2nd millenium BC, of the island at a later date and, under the same name or as Leucas, the island's chief town as late as the Byzantine period (13th century).

We can see traces of the town's historical continuity and prosperity in its Cyclopean walls (at the spot known as Kouloumos), arches, water tanks, sections of an aqueduct, and pre-Roman theatre —all discovered by Dörpfeld— and in the remains of Byzantine walls and towers.

Whatever the earthquakes and seven centuries of neglect have left of the town can still be seen, but requires patient searching among the farms and fields.

There are also traces of two ancient roads, leading west from Nericus/Leucas to the port of Heraeion, on what is today the bay of Ai-Yannis. It may be these roads which gave the modern town of Lefkada the name 'Amaxiki' (carriage-road) after the 18 th century.

4 km: we continue southwards on the main road, reaching **Karyotes,** where the last remaining salt-pans in Lefkada can be seen (signpost, left).

The production of salt was once among the main sources of income for the island, and the **salt-pans** stretched much further north than they do today. After the earthquakes, a considerable part of the southern side of Lefkada town was rebuilt on what had once been salt-pans. This can be seen in old photographs.

The salt-pans are also a good viewpoint for seeing how the system of fortifications to defend the Lefkada channel was laid out.

To the north, we can see the fort of Santa Maura blocking off the entrance, and the **Modern Fort** or **Grivas Fort** covering the landward side. The southern end of the channel was protected by a little Venetian fortress called the Fortino. In 1808, in order to cope with Ali Pasha, who had built the **St George Fort** on the mainland coast opposite, the Russians strengthened the Fortino and called it Fort Alexander in honour of Tsar Alexander I. The same name was also given to the harbour of Drepano, which lay to the south of the modern port of Lefkada. Lastly, on the left-hand side as we come up from the south is little Fort Constantine, also built by the Russians. It was named in honour of the brother of Alexander I, Grand Duke Constantine.

Towards the end of the village of Karyotes is a turning to the right for **Katouna**, a village which tourism has not touched. The route (3 km) is a very pretty one, and would make a nice walk.

The road climbs steadily but never particularly steeply, and there is a most attractive view across to the mainland. The landscape as we head for the interior of the island is also attractive, with olives and cypresses clothing folds in the terrain and the higher hills in the background.

When we arrive in Katouna, it turns out to be much larger than one would have expected, with charming little alleys through which to wander.

5 km: the road to Nidri, along which most of the tourist traffic is concentrated, now reaches **Lygia** with its little fishing harbour. This is where the British made their first landing on 9 March 1810, soon overcoming French resistance and advancing to capture Lefkada town.

9 km: Nikiana. This is an area rather than a clearly marked village with a centre and suburbs. It was first settled by villagers from the upland community of Alexandros (see p. 109), to which there is a road up the hill. Among the dense woods which line the road are numerous tourist facilities, with pleasant accommodation and a full range of services.

Even when the tourist season is at its height, the Lygia-Nikiana area is relatively quiet, despite the large number of visitors. There are good but narrow beaches all the way along the coast.

However, the main attraction of this area is its landscape. The view across the channel to mainland Greece is magical, while after Nikiana the hills on our right become higher and come closer and closer to the sea. A little further south we get our first glimpse of the islands off Nidri, which we shall be describing below.

From Nikiana, a road (which needs care because it is narrow) leads up to Alexandros (p.109). It climbs very steeply away from the sea above Nikiana.

14 km: we reach **Periyali**, with its fine beach, which is used by many visitors from Nidri.

Access to the mountain, with its superb views over Nidri and the surrounding area, takes the form of a minor road leading out of Periyali: it begins at the little blue sign marked 'Platystoma' and 'Karya', and turns left at the school. Although steep, there is no particular difficulty about this road. After about 10 kilometres, it reaches Platystoma.

Every fisherman has his day on the dock at Lygia.

Nikiana from above.

17 km: Shortly after Periyali we enter **Nidri**.

This was the first village on Lefkada to attract tourism and for at least the last ten years has been very busy in the summer. Now it is a proper holiday resort, full of bustle and life. Yet despite the crowds of people —and the traffic along the main street— the natural beauty of Nidri will always be a source of attraction to visitors.

Nidri is arranged in rather a peculiar manner. A line of buildings stands along the front, housing cafes, restaurants and tavernas on the side facing the sea, while on the side facing the road the same buildings are shops. The quay itself can be reached from the north end or through an archway approximately half-way along the main street.

Once on the quay, one realises at once why Nidri is so popular.

It really is a sort of encapsulation of Greek island holidays, with all the vi-

A unique landscape. Nydri, Mado

tality and pleasure which that implies. The view across the bay is superb.

The quay in front of the cafes is lined with yachts, fishing-boats and other vessels; out at sea, the pedalos come and go, while windsurfers and water-skiers swoop by. Off to the left, swimmers enjoy the water off the calm and sandy beach.

It was at Nidri that, according to Dörpfeld, Homer's Odysseus had his capital. The excavations of the Ger-man archaeologist to the south of the village brought to light traces of in-habitation in the Middle Helladic pe-riod (1900-1550 BC): tombs with a variety of funerary offerings, pottery, etc. and an aqueduct and other items from the Mycenean age. Roman and —perhaps— Byzantine tombs were also found.

There are schools which teach sea sports, and all the equipment neces-sary for them can be rented in Nidri.

ırpios and Meganisi to the rear.

As we stand on the quay at Nidri, we face the end of the peninsula which forms Vlycho Bay. On this stands the chapel of St Kyriake, and a little above it, Dörpfeld's tomb (see below). Further out are the islands: Sparti to the left, Madouri a little closer in, and Skorpios in the background (see p. 128). To the right are the quiet waters of Vlycho, an outstanding natural harbour and beauty spot. Behind it is an imposing range of mountains: the hills above Periyali to the north, Mt Stavrotas (with the island's highest peak) in the centre, and, to the south west, the summit above Vlycho.

The sunset at Nidri is another of the factors which make the place unforgettable. The upland mass of the island stands on one side, with its olive groves and expanses of forest, while on the other the sea and the land mingle, with almost landlocked coves and a sea like a mirror going together to create a landscape of unique beauty. When the sun sinks behind the mountains, the light spreads out, enveloping everything in its magic reflection.

However, over and above its natural beauty, Nidri also has all the amenities of a modern resort town to offer visitors. There are plenty of places to stay, restaurants, shops, banks, a post office and all the other facilities.

The night-life, although relatively subdued, is also interesting, and the cafes and bars along the front are busy until late into the night.

The Lefkada Festival, though centring on Lefkada town itself, also 'decentralises' some of its concerts and other events to Nidri, and these attract lively interest on the part of Greek and foreign visitors.

It is certain that a visit to Nidri and its surroundings will have more in store for visitors than we are able to describe here. However, we give below some ideas for things to see and do in the vicinity.

Peaceful moments on the outskirts of cosmopolitan Nidri.

The bay of Vlychos and Nydri to the rear.

Short Trips from Nidri

1. The waterfall

One of the prettiest trips from Nidri —and also one of the shortest, making a walk of about 45 minutes through most attractive scenery— will bring us to something rather unexpected: a waterfall!

We take the road signposted 'Rachi' near the end of the main street at the north end of the village and immediately enter an area of orchards and olive groves in the little plain behind Nidri to the west; this was once the area's main source of wealth. We soon come to the small village of Rachi, which has a hotel. The name means 'ridge' and it is easy to see how it came to be given to this village perched on top of a rock.

Here the road forks and we follow the signpost, to the right. The road soon narrows to a track and loses its surface, becoming a path after a further 15 minutes and climbing along the side of the Dimosari gorge. The walls gradually close in, and the path ends at a group of enormous rocks between which the water rushes down, forming a series of little waterfalls. In the summer heat this is a wonderfully cool place, although there is much more water in the springtime. This walk through the gardens is well worth the effort for what lies at the end of it.

Those who have some means of transport can travel on in this direction to visit Karya and the other mountain villages described in Route35.

To get on to the Vafkeri road, we turn sharp left in Rachi and take the lower of the two roads in front of us (the other is a dead end). When we have climbed high enough on the hillside, there is a superb view across Nidri and out to the islands. Vafkeri is 7 km from Rachi and a similar distance from Karya.

These villages are described in more detail in Route 3.

Unexpected spots high on the hilside around Rachi.

2. To the Chapel of St Kyriake

This tour round Vlycho Bay is much longer than the walk to the waterfall, and although most of the route is in shade, many people will prefer to take some form of transport rather than walk.

We head south, leaving Nidri. After passing the site of Dörpfeld's excavations (see p. 113), we come out on to the seafront again at **Vlycho**, an attractive little village squeezed in between the sea and the mountainside. It is famous for its boatyards, which are among the last in Greece still to construct boats in the traditional manner. The skill of these craftsmen is in great demand; orders flood in and there are long waiting-lists.

After Vlycho, we fork left at the signpost for Desimi. The road runs downhill among ancient olive trees at the head of the bay, and soon comes to another crossroads. This is the beginning of the area known as **Yeni** and renowned for its beauty. If we go straight ahead, we will come to **Desimi**, where there is a beach and a camp site.

But the road to the left continues round the bay and is a lovely walk under the olive trees, with views across the water, first to Vlycho and then to Nidri, with Mt Stavrotas looming in the background.

The road ends at a sort of car-park, from which a path leads on (to the left) and in five minutes brings us to the **Chapel of St Kyriake.**

Yeni is protected because of its natural beauty.

Nidri is now directly opposite. On the top of the hill, inside the garden of what was his house, is Dörpfeld's tomb. The whole area is pretty and shady with a fine view: an ideal place to sit and watch the yachts and fishing-boats coming and going from Nidri.

On the way back to Nidri, we can stop for refreshment at one of the attractive cafes on the side of the road towards the bay.

3. To Palaiokatouna and Niochori

The road to Niochori (signposted from the main street in Nidri) climbs gently up from the fine olive groves and orchards in the plain of Nidri (described above) before coming first to **Palaiokatouna**, after about two kilometres. From here there is a view over Nidri, the wooded islands, and the mountains of Akarnania in the background.

However, keen walkers have a further treat in store if they decide to keep on climbing as far as Niochori (2.5 km of track after Palaiokatouna).

Niochori is almost deserted; the shepherds who once lived here moved down to Palaiokatouna and Nidri years ago, abandoning their houses, which are gradually falling to pieces.

The track continues to climb, and after passing close to the ruined monastery of the Archangels (Ayii Asomati) leads to Englouvi.

Both Palaiokatouna and Niochori have old churches with wall-paintings.

St Kyriake, opposite Nidri.

Out to the Islands

There are two ways of visiting the islands off Nidri. The first is by caique from Nidri; trips of varying lengths are available, sailing to all or only some of the following places: the Papanikoli cave, Ayios Ioannis beach on Meganisi for a swim (or, depending on the weather, on the Lefkadan beach facing it), lunch at Meganisi, a trip around Skorpios (the local boatmen are inexhaustible sources of stories about the Onassis family) and a dip in the sea (from the caique) in one of the bays around Skorpios.

These trips start from the quay at Nidri (information from the travel agencies) and one should ask around to be sure of getting just the right combination of visits.

The other way is to take the ferry to Meganisi, which of course passes Skorpios. This means that one is not bound by the choices or whims of the boatman or one's fellow-passengers. There are regular sailings for Meganisi all the year round (the island's older children go to school on Lefkada) and the trip to Vathy takes about 45 minutes.

For those interested in longer trips, there are sailings from Nidri for Cephallonia and Ithaki.

Departures are much more frequent in the summer, of course, but even in winter the ferries go twice a week. Information from the ticket agency, on the main street of Nidri.

The Valaoritis house on Madouri.

Madouri

This is the island nearest to Nidri, lying only 800 metres off the coast. It is densely wooded, and on it stands the house of the great poet Aristotelis Valaoritis (see p. 47). The island is privately-owned and landing is not allowed.

Skorpios

This is another privately-owned and forbidden island. It lies 3 miles off Nidri, and its renown is bound up with the happiest —and most tragic— moments in the story of its owners, the Onassis family.

The feelings of the locals towards the Onassis family are rather mixed. On the one hand, they undoubtedly brought jobs and money to Nidri: many of the islanders worked on Skorpios, and some still do. But in its desire to protect its peace and privacy, the family used its influence to put a stop to any tourist development for many years. It was only after the death of Aristotle Onassis that the people of Nidri were really able to decide about their own fates.

As we have said, it is forbidden to land on Skorpios, but a trip by caique around the island gives some idea of the luxury in which its owners lived. Scattered around amongst the thick greenery which cloaks the island are houses, tavernas, farm buildings, jetties and even a heliport.

The security guards make themselves very conspicuous and the warning signs are to be given very serious attention.

The enchanting little island of Skorpios.

Meganisi

The size of this island is reflected in its name (meaning 'big island'). It lies 4 miles to the south west of Nidri.

Meganisi is not really like Lefkada at all; one gets the impression that it happened just by chance to end up next to its bigger neighbour.

This is a seafaring island, and many of the men are absent at sea for months on end. Its traditional society has hardly been touched by the outside world, but the islanders are very hospitable and friendly towards visitors. The island's three villages have some limited facilities for coping with the tourist trade.

Although Karia is the place known for its embroidery, the women of Meganisi (and indeed of lots of other places around Lefkada) are rarely to be seen without some piece of embroidery in their hands. They also make strips of lace to adorn the traditional local costume.

Anyone who wishes to see much of Meganisi and its three interesting villages will have to have transport or be prepared to do quite a bit of walking.

The ferry from Nidri calls first at the little harbour below Spartochori (see below). The road up to the village is very steep and twisting, and those with cars would be better to avoid it.

The second stop is at **Vathy**, a picturesque little village huddled around its harbour. This is a quiet spot, with excellent fish tavernas. A path leads from the somewhat neglected swing park over the hill behind the village (10 minutes) to a deserted bay where there is a camp site with reed huts.

The surfaced road (approx. 1 km) leads south from Vathy to **Katomeri.** This charming, traditional village is a labyrinth of narrow alleyways, in the midst of which is the only petrol station on the island.

Despite its isolation, Katomeri is an unexpectedly lively place. In the evening, the streets and cafes fill up and visitors are made to feel very welcome.

A road leads out of Katomeri to the east, past the petrol station, and takes us to the long, narrow and quiet bay of **Atherino**.

It then continues as far as the tip of Cape Akoni. The bay is used as a yacht anchorage.

The other road from Katomeri (straight up through the middle of the village) goes to **Spartochori** (4 km), the largest village on the island. This is another maze of little alleys, but by way of contrast to Katomeri, Spartochori gives the impression of having seen better days.

A track leads west from Spartochori to the beach of Ayios Ioannis (4 km), thus completing the island's network of roads. The rest of Meganisi is road-less, though there are paths everywhere.

The sight which most tourists will remember from Meganisi is the Daimonas or Papanikolis cave, on the south west coast. After the surrender of Greece to the Germans in April 1941, the submarine *Papanikolis* hid in this huge cave and used it as a base for carrying on operations against the occupying forces. A visit to the cave forms part of many caique trips, and, depending on the boldness of the captain, the caique will either enter the cave or simply sail close to its entrance.

The Papanikolis Cave on Meganisi.

ROUTE 5

Nidri - Poros - Syvota - Vasiliki - Syvros - Ayios Petros

We follow Route 3 as far as Nidri. Heading south, we pass the site of Dörpfeld's excavations and reach the start of Route 5, which will take us to the coves and bays of southern Lefkada.

In effect, routes 4 and 5 parts of the same itinerary along the eastern and southern coast's because of the interesting spots in the vicinity of Nidri and Vasiliki.

After Vlycho the road begins to climb, with a wonderful view back to Nidri and Vlycho Bay.

The tower at Poros.

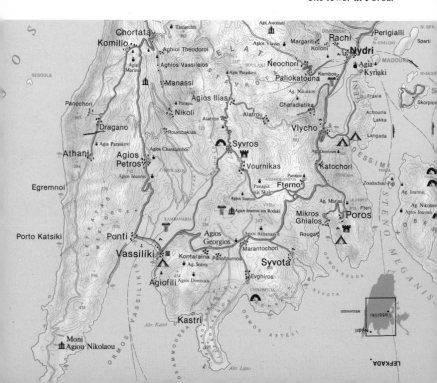

22 km: As we climb, we pass two turnings to **Katochori**, a very attractive village with stone-built houses. Nestling in against the hillside, it is rather as if Katochori had decided to turn its back on Nidri. The road up to the village is a good place to see, on the hillside opposite, the combination of olives and cypresses which is so characteristic of the Ionian Islands and which has attracted so many painters to them.

25 km: A turning, left, off the main road will bring us in 2 km to **Poros.** This is another attractive village, close to the sea and yet almost unspoiled. It stands on rather an unusual site, facing west with its back to the sea. Given that the hillside on which Poros is built is rather steep, a stroll through its alleys can be an exhausting business, but the attractive houses are a reward for one's efforts. There is a popular religious (and secular) feast here on 6 December, St Nicholas' day, with music, dancing and much eating and drinking.

Above the village, at an altitude of about 800 metres, are the remains of a tower which was presumably erected there to keep watch over the area. According to Dörpfeld, the tower —and the olive press which stands near it— date from the 4th century BC.

The road up from the car park at the entrance to the village provides us with an opportunity for a pleasant walk up to the chapel on the hill-top. A track then descends into the fields from which the villagers of Poros make their living and continues, as a path, through a peaceful agricultural landscape with a fine view over the channel which separates Lefkada

View of Poros.

from Meganisi and the other islands. The two peaks which can be seen behind Meganisi are those of Kalamos and Arkoudi (on the right; Ithaki can sometimes be seen far in the distance in the same direction). In the centre is the islet of Atokos.

28 km: Poros itself does not have much in the way of tourist facilities, but the narrow road we encounter on our right as soon as we enter the village runs down to the excellent beach at **Rouda Bay** (otherwise known as **Mikros Yalos**).

This is a magical place, particularly suited to fishing and bathing. There is a camp site with its own restaurant and shop (it also rents cabins). In summer, tavernas operate along the beach and also to the left, in the direction of the little jetty. The beauty of the combination of colours in the white pebbles,

the deep blue water and the fringe of olive trees is truly unforgettable. The track along the south side of Rouda Bay leads round the cape to Syvota.

We return to the Poros turning on the main road, which now heads for Vasiliki, running first west, high above the sea, and then south.

27 km: At the point where the road changes direction, we come to a crossroads. The turning to the right goes through Vournikas and Syvros (see below) before ending in Vasiliki. From this road, another turning (not far from the crossroads) heads north for the unspoiled hamlet of **Fterno**, an idyllic place with a superb view across to Poros and down to Rouda Bay.

We take the left fork, which is also the main road south.

31 km: A turning (left) off the main road takes us in 2 km to Syvota.

Fishermen at Mikros Yalos.

A panoramic view of Poros.

The beautiful beach of Mikros Yialos.

Syvota stands at the head of a fjord-like bay which penetrates deep into the land, twisting and turning, and is an outstanding natural harbour. The water is calm and warm, and for that reason it is a favourite place for the yacht flotillas to be encountered more and more frequently in the Ionian Islands. Indeed, many yachts are laid up for the winter at Syvota.

Apart from its natural beauty, Syvota can also boast what are probably the best fish tavernas on Lefkada, along the sea-front. Most of these have their own jetties, which are mostly used for off-loading catches of fish. The fishing and taverna businesses employ most of the members of the few families who are resident here. Those arriving by sea, of course, can tie up at one of the jetties and will find themselves only a few steps from the various delights available in the tavernas. Since this is a very popular place, attracting not only people from the town but also many foreign visitors, some of the tavernas are open all the year round.

Rooms can be rented at Syvota. There is a small beach, on the north side of the bay.

We return to the main road junction and continue west through an increasingly agricultural landscape, with the plain of Vasiliki now visible in the distance. The next landmark is the turning for Evyiros.

34 km: Evyiros is known principally for the fact that to the south of the village is the Hirospilia cave, where Dörpfeld found traces of human habitation dating from be-

The deep bay of Syvota.

tween the Neolithic age and the historical period. His finds are now in a small museum in Nidri.

35 km: After the turning for Evyiros we come to **Marandochori**, a farming community which straggles along the roadside. Nearby, at the spot known as Bisa, is a little **Monastery of St George**, built in the 16th century. Only the monastery church has survived, with good wall-paintings which have been damaged by being whitewashed over, and a small but interesting 18th century wooden screen.

A side-road leads from Marandochori to **Kastri** (5 km, signpost). The road is poor but the trip is worth the effort, because Kastri has an excellent beach.

The landscape is delightful, and there is a camp site nearby.

Syvota, an ideal anchorage for yachts..

40 km: We continue along the main road and, after passing the turning (right) for Syvros and Ayios Ilias, reach Vasiliki.

Vasiliki and Nidri are the two most popular resorts on Lefkada, and they have some points in common. Both stand at the head of bays, with intensively-cultivated plains behind them and mountains rising in the distance. But while Nidri spreads out along its beach, Vasiliki is clustered round its little harbour, shaded by eucalyptus and plane trees, which is the centre of

life in the village. The feast of Our Lady, on 15 August, is the occasion for particular celebrations in Vasiliki.

In recent years, Vasiliki has developed into a self-contained tourist resort with a full range of facilities. Accommodation of all kinds is available, from rented rooms to hotels, and there is a large and modern camp site along the beach a little way. The harbour is lined with restaurants and cafes, while the main street —leading north from the harbour— has all the shops one could possibly want.

For swimming, Vasiliki has a sandy beach some 2 km long to the north west of the village.

The night life is vigorous, with discos for those who like their holidays to be a little more lively. Visitors who want a quieter time will find the seafront cafes, which are open until late at night, a pleasant place to sit.

The road (which later becomes a path) along the harbour to the south leads to a number of little coves which are good places for swimming. These bays end at the exceptionally good beach of **Ayiofylli**, which can only be reached by sea (there is a caique service from Vasiliki harbour).

A long beach at Vasiliki, and the bay, superb for windsurfing.

One could also walk over to Kastri, which would take about two hours, to swim there, but then of course one would have to walk all the way back as well.

Vasiliki Bay is an ideal spot for wind-surfing, and has begun to attract more and more devotees of the sport in recent years. All day the wind-surfers with their multi-coloured sails can be seen criss-crossing the blue waters of the bay. In the mornings, there is a sea breeze which makes sailing safe for beginners, while in the afternoon the wind often rises to strengths which will challenge the more experienced.

Those who do not have their own wind-surfing equipment will find they can hire it at the beach.

Ayiofylli can be reached by boat form Vasiliki.

Short trips from Vasiliki

There are daily caique sailings for Porto Katsiki (round Cape Lefkatas, with its awesome cliffs, see p. 102) and Ayiofylli beach. Less frequently, the caiques go to other destinations: whole-day trips to the Papanikolis cave and Meganisi, Skorpios and elsewhere. Information about these trips can be obtained at the harbour itself (most of the caiques have placards advertising their sailings) or from one of the travel agencies.

Those with their own transport may prefer to visit Porto Katsiki and Cape Lefkatas by land.

From Vasiliki, we take the road which runs along behind the beach. Where the beach comes to an end, at the settlement called **Ponti,** we turn north and climb up to the large village of Ayios Petros, 8 km from Vasiliki.

48 km: Ayios Petros. This is a primarily agricultural community with a fine view to the south, and below, over Vasiliki, and up to the impressive summits of Mt Stavrotas to the north east.

From Ayios Petros, the turning at Komilio for Athani and Porto Katsiki is 8 km away. After Komilio, we follow Route 2 (see p. 99).

Bell-tower at Ayios Petros.

Another interesting trip —particularly on warm summer evenings— is to Ayios Ilias. As we head north, we will cross the verdant plain of Vasiliki and climb up into the hills, where the cooler air of the mountains and a fine view await us.

We take the main road back towards Nidri and shortly after the end of Vasiliki turn left for Syvros. The road dips down into the fields, giving us an opportunity to see how farming is carried out in Lefkada, with seasonal crops being sown in among and under the olive trees to increase the farmer's

income. The Vasiliki area also culti-
vates flowers, whose seeds are exported.

The road continues in a northerly
direction, through the lush landscape
up a number of steep bends, before
entering **Syvros**.

This pretty village is still a predom-
inantly farming community. There is
a long and rather narrow main street,
with a few shops, cafes and restaurants, followed by a large paved square
with a view down across the plain.

The road turning to the right leads
to Vournikas and to the spot known as
Rodaki, on the hilltop which domi-
nates the area, where there is a ruined
Monastery of St John. The monastery
church is all that has survived, built
on the floor of what must have been a
large ancient temple. The site is worth
a visit not only for the fine view over
the plain of Vasiliki but also for the
paintings on the east wall of the
church, which have survived in good
condition.

The turning for **Ayios Ilias** is on the
other side of the road from the square.
The road twists higher and higher up
the mountainside, in a landscape
which gradually becomes more and
more barren. By the time we reach
Ayios Ilias (6 km), the vegetation has
all but disappeared.

The contrast with the bare mountainside makes the plants and flowers
with which the courtyards of the village houses are crammed even more
welcome.

At an altitude of 620 metres, Ayios
Ilias is the second-highest village on
the island, and it has a superb view
down over the plain and far out to sea.
When the air is clear, Cephallonia and
Ithaki can be seen in the distance.

There were two reasons for building
some villages high on the mountainside. The first was that certain crops
—wheat, for instance— needed to be
quite high up in order to grow properly, while the flocks of sheep and
goats were brought up here for summer grazing.

The second reason —and the more
important one— was that these mountain villages were ideal places to take
refuge from the attacks of the pirates
who harried the whole of Greece in the
Middle Ages. As soon as the warning
arrived that a raid was imminent, the
inhabitants of the lower parts made for
Ayios Ilias, carrying with them whatever they could, and they hid there
until the danger was past.

Apart from making the acquaintance of an attractive village, there is
also another reason for visiting Ayios
Ilias. This is the starting-point for the
ascent of Mt Stavrotas, the highest
peak on the island at 1,141 metres. The
path begins towards the top of the
village, but those thinking of undertaking the climb should probably con-
sult local wisdom before setting out.

Here we complete our tour of the
lovely island of Lefkada, the island
which has inspired Greek and foreign
poets, since ancient times. We would
like to think that this little guidebook
has been the strting-point for your acquaintance with an island that belongs
as much to the mainland as it does to
the Ionian, and that it will have stimu-
lated you to discover all the singular
and beautiful features of its natural
and human world.

BIBLIOGRAPHY

ΕΓΚΥΚΛΟΠΑΙΔΕΙΑ ΔΟΜΗ: s.v. Λευκάς.

ΚΟΝΤΟΜΙΧΗ ΠΑΝΤΑΖΗ: Η λαϊκή ιατρική στη Λευκάδα, Εκδόσεις ΓΡΗΓΟΡΗ, Αθήνα 1985.

ΚΟΝΤΟΜΙΧΗ ΠΑΝΤΑΖΗ: Τα γεωργικά της Λευκάδας, Εκδόσεις ΓΡΗΓΟΡΗ, Αθήνα 1985.

ΣΠ. ΒΛΑΝΤΗ: Η νήσος Λευκάς και αι πόλεις αυτής ανά τους αιώνας, Αθήνα 1915.

ΣΠ. ΒΛΑΝΤΗ: Η Λευκάς από τους Φράγκους, Τούρκους, Ενετούς 1204-1797, Λευκάδα 1902.

ΓΕΡ. ΜΑΥΡΟΓΙΑΝΝΗ: Ιστορία των Ιονίων νήσων 1797-1815, Αθήνα 1889

ΚΩΝΣΤ. Γ. ΜΑΧΑΙΡΑ: Το εν Λευκάδι Φρούριων της Αγίας Μαύρας, Αθήνα 1956.

Αφιέρωμα στη Λευκάδα, 1979, Φυσιολ. Σύνδεσμος Πειραιώς ΖΗΝΩΝ

Π. Γ. ΡΟΝΤΟΓΙΑΝΝΗ: Ιστορία της Λευκάδος, τ. Α' και Β', Αθήνα 1982.

Επετηρίδα Εταιρείας Λευκαδικών Μελετών, τ 1 (1971), τ 3 (1974)

ΔΡΑΚΟΝΤΑΕΙΔΗΣ ΓΕΡΑΣ.: «Σύντομη Ιστορία Λευκάδος καί λαογραφία Αγίου Πέτρου», Αθήνα 1970.

ΜΑΛΑΚΑΣΗΣ ΔΗΜΟΣ: «Τα παλιά σπίτια της Λευκάδας», Αθήνα 1984.

ΜΑΜΑΛΟΥΚΑΣ ΤΑΚΗΣ: «Λαογραφικά της Λευκάδας», ΟΔΕΒ, Αθήνα, 1978.

Κ. ΜΑΧΑΙΡΑ: Ναοί και Μοναί της Λευκάδος, Αθήνα 1957, «Βαλαωρίτης, 1824-1879», Εκδ. Εταιρείας Λευκαδικών Μελετών, Αθήνα 1975.

«Άγγελος Σικελιανός 1884-1951, βίος, έργα, ανθολογία, κριτική, εικόνες, βιβ/φία», Εκδ. Εταιρείας Λευκαδικών Μελετών, Αθήνα 1971.

Format: 17 × 24 cm.

GREEK COOKERY & Wines

Available in 15 languages

ᴀ luxury edition which takes us into the magical world of Greek and Cypriot cuisine with traditional recipes, local specialities, pastries, wines and other beverages, from all the areas of Greece and Cyprus, each recipe with the estimated number of calories.